10 MINUTE GUIDE

Macmillan USA
201 West 103rd Street
Indianapolis, IN 46290

A Pearson Education Company

George J. Kops

10 MINUTE GUIDE TO BUSINESS PRESENTATIONS

Contents

Introduction

Presenting effectively can be a demanding task for many in the business world. Preparation time is often short, the information needed may not be complete, the objectives can be unclear, and you may be extremely nervous about the whole process. As a result, the talk may not be as effective as you and your listeners would like. The *10 Minute Guide to Business Presentations* is designed to provide you with the information you need to make your presentations much better than they may have been in the past. Each 10-minute lesson provides the essential information to make that particular segment of your presentation more effective. By completing the work sheets in Appendix B, "The Speakers Notebook," you'll be ensured a full understanding of the concepts before you put them into practice.

In addition, this book makes use of three icons that help you to find the information you need:

TIP

> Tip icons give you a different perspective on what has been said, to get you thinking.

PLAIN ENGLISH

> Plain English icons provide definitions of terms that might be new to you.

CAUTION

> Caution icons warn you of potentially tricky or dangerous pitfalls.

When you've completed the book you'll be more knowledgeable and better able to deliver effective business presentations to your peers, supervisors, and the customers your company serves. As you become more skilled you'll be a better professional and a more valuable contributor to your company.

Improving your presentation skills is a worthwhile pursuit that will only result in better things happening for you.

Good luck, and let me know if there are any questions I can help you with.

ABOUT THE AUTHOR

George J. Kops founded Focus Communications International in 1985. The company works with clients to improve their communications skills, enabling them to become more effective communicators and better able to persuade. The wide range of clients George has worked with have successfully used his methods to improve their oral and written presentation skills, which has helped them to advance their careers and business enterprises through better personal communications.

George Kops can be reached by phone at 203-966-0282, by fax at 203-966-1949, and by e-mail at www.kops@focuscommunications.com.

ACKNOWLEDGMENTS

I would like to thank Dick Worth for all of his help in making this possible, as well as Bob Callaway, Al Reams, and Richard Southern for their many contributions to our training and to the thousands of graduates who have participated in our programs.

Lesson 1
Become an Effective Speaker

In this lesson you learn about the importance of effective public speaking and about several skill sets that will make you a better presenter.

A young manager once told me that he'd started to move up in his organization only after he'd overcome his fear of public speaking. It had always scared him to death. Once he mastered those feelings he began to work on developing his speaking skills, and found out that he was actually a very good presenter.

Stand Up and Speak

One of the best ways to turn public speaking into a more positive experience is to consider all the advantages you bring to the table:

- You probably know more than anyone in the audience about your topic.

- If you leave something out or forget something, the audience will never know. Remember, they didn't know what you were planning to say in the first place.

- Most listeners would much rather be sitting where they are than standing where you are. So they feel for you and empathize with your situation.

- The audience usually wants you to succeed; they're in your corner, not rooting against you.

- Many other people in the room probably wish that they could do what you're doing, so relax and enjoy being a star.

You undoubtedly have more going for you than you think.

ACKNOWLEDGE THE PERSUASIVENESS OF PRESENTATIONS

When Carleton Fiorina took over as CEO of Hewlett-Packard (HP), which had recently fallen on hard times, the first thing she did was to start communicating with her employees. She traveled to work sites around the globe and addressed more than 20 large meetings in 10 different countries. The new CEO had an important message to deliver, which involved revitalizing HP and making it successful; the means she chose was oral communication.

Whether you're the CEO of a large organization or the supervisor of a small work team, you must know how to communicate effectively. When you stand up to speak, you instantly become a voice of authority and your audience is waiting to hear what you have to say. The words you use can have several purposes. They can

- **Inform.** Sometimes you only want to give your audience information. For example, you may want to tell them about the past week's production figures or the results of your meetings with several important customers.

- **Explain.** Perhaps the purpose of your talk is to briefly explain a new process or procedure, like how to file a health insurance claim or conduct a performance evaluation. Generally, talks that explain also provide information.

TIP

Many speakers believe that they are simply presenting information. In reality, they want their listeners to use that information to take action, so their talks are actually persuasive. It's important to know your purpose when you stand up to speak.

- **Persuade.** These are usually the most difficult types of presentations. Carleton Fiorina, for example, was trying to persuade her employees to make a change in their organization. Speakers like Fiorina usually use information and explanation in the service of persuasion.

If you are clear in your purpose, it's easier to organize your presentation and to deliver it.

USE PERSUASIVE TALKS REGULARLY

Most persuasive talks do not involve changing the direction of a major corporation. Nor are you likely to be put in the position of Winston Churchill who used his words and distinctive speaking style to help convince the British people to keep fighting during the dark days of World War II. Nevertheless, your presentation could make a significant difference.

While the world may not move from a state of war to a state of peace, your department or business unit may make an important change. Perhaps it will decide to embark on a quality improvement process or enter a new consumer market or streamline its R&D procedures. As the person who suggested this change, you have an unusual opportunity:

- To make an impact on your organization and change the minds of employees.

- To stand out and be remembered as the person who advocated a new direction.

- To advance your own career within your department or company.

Take advantage of opportunities to speak effectively about changes and developments you've initiated to those who will be affected by them.

TRIUMPH OVER STAGE FRIGHT

What runs through your mind when you think about public speaking? Perhaps you remember an incident from your childhood when you appeared in a school play and forgot one of your lines. Or you may recall standing in front of an audience at a PTA meeting and looking at 100 eyes that seemed to be staring back at you—and staring and staring and staring.

It's enough to send chills up and down the spine of even the most courageous person. Indeed, most people admit that they'd rather do anything than give a presentation. And that includes root canal procedures, getting fired from a job, and even dying.

Stage fright is a normal feeling for anybody who has to get up in front of an audience. Even great actors suffer from it.

PLAIN ENGLISH

> **Stage fright** is a natural anxiety that most people feel when they get up and speak before a large group of listeners.

There's an old saying that *he who hesitates is lost.* The same may be said for anyone who is afraid to get up and speak. The people who move ahead in an organization are the same ones who seem capable of distinguishing themselves from their colleagues. Often this means that they know how to get up on their feet and deliver a clear, persuasive message.

If you can give a powerful talk, not only can it catch the attention of your listeners, it can focus much of that attention on you, showcasing your ideas and showing your listeners that you are someone who knows how to be a leader.

CAUTION

> Don't fire before you aim. A successful talk will help you stand out, but an unsuccessful one could damage you. Make sure you've thought about what you want to say before you start speaking.

AIM FOR A MEMORABLE PRESENTATION

A young engineer once told me that many of the meetings he was attending were becoming depressingly similar. Employees would sit down, listen to the speaker for a few brief moments, then begin doodling and daydreaming. It seems extremely impolite, until you remember how many meetings some people must attend in the course of a day and how excessively dull the speakers usually seem to be.

Most of us have learned to accept a pretty low level of performance in business presentations. After all, you tell yourself, the topic is usually not very scintillating; what else can you expect? But every once in a while, you hear a speaker who is far better than average. Suddenly your expectations are raised again, and you remind yourself of what's actually possible.

Once I heard a speaker deliver a presentation that he routinely gave to new salespeople who had been hired by his organization. He spoke about five different types of customers and how to convince them to buy his product. I've never forgotten that presentation because of the effective way it was delivered. I demand the same things from myself whenever I speak. Here are my six rules:

1. Make the message clear so no one will misunderstand what you're saying.

2. Sound as if you mean it; so many speakers seem to have very little interest in what they're saying.

3. Be yourself. Don't try to play a part or mimic the mannerisms of another speaker. It won't work.

4. Personalize the presentation. Let your personality stand out and put its stamp on what you're saying.

5. Connect with your listeners. Try to turn the presentation into a one-on-one experience for them.

 TIP

> Think about presentations that made a strong impact on you. Taking the point of view of an audience member, expect of yourself the kind of presentation you would hope to hear.

6. Tell the audience why they're there and why they should listen to you; otherwise they won't.

Follow these six rules and you're on your way to delivering memorable presentations.

SPEAK POWERFULLY ON ANY OCCASION

You may be asked to speak in a variety of situations. Sometimes you'll be given plenty of notice and have an opportunity to prepare; sometimes you won't. You'll be required to speak almost on the spur of the moment. In each case, you should try to make a powerful impression on your audience.

STREAMLINE YOUR INTRODUCTIONS TO SPEAKERS

Perhaps you're not the main speaker for an event but have been asked to introduce someone who will give the keynote address. Here are several elements to remember when you give your introduction:

- **Keep it short.** Remember that they've come to hear someone else—not you. Forty-five seconds to a minute is long enough.

- **Introduce the title or topic of the talk.** That's the thing most listeners want to hear first.

- **Relate the speaker's topic to the group.** Explain how it's relevant to the listeners so they'll pay attention.

- **Describe the speaker.** Discuss his or her qualifications to speak on the subject.

- **Tell the audience the speaker's name, and sit down.**

The speaker will be grateful, and so will the audience.

Present Awards with Style

You may be asked to speak at a retirement dinner or present an award to an individual or team for an outstanding accomplishment. Remember the following key guidelines:

- Be brief but not so brief that you are too vague about the recipient's unique characteristics.

- Give legitimate, honest praise but don't overdo it.

- Specifically mention what the recipient has done and why the recognition is being given.

- Personalize your presentation so it doesn't sound as if it could apply to anyone.

- Prepare for your talk by gathering information about the recipient of the recognition or award.

TIP

Learn about the person you're recognizing from published information and from colleagues and friends.

Giving recognition is an important role. These guidelines will ensure that you do it with distinction.

BE AN ORGANIZED MEETING FACILITATOR

Most of us spend too much time in meetings because they usually seem very poorly planned. Generally the leader or facilitator does not have a clear program in mind for the meeting. If you are the facilitator, remember the following:

1. Try to accomplish only one objective and be clear with participants about what that objective will be.

2. Carefully lay out the *agenda* at the beginning of the meeting.

PLAIN ENGLISH

An **agenda** is a list of things to be decided or acted on at a meeting.

3. Set a firm time limit on the meeting and try to keep it short.

4. Come to clear decisions and action items at the end of a meeting. Otherwise nothing will ever get accomplished. Remember these guidelines and you'll keep your meeting focused and action oriented.

PREPARE AND REHEARSE FORMAL PRESENTATIONS

Sometimes you're asked to give a formal presentation in front of a large group. Each of the chapters in this book contains detailed information that will help you with this type of presentation. For now, here are a few general guidelines to keep in mind:

- **Prepare.** This can't be stated too strongly. Too many speakers leave their preparation until the last minute.

- **Keep it simple.** Don't overwhelm your audience with information just because you have it at your fingertips. They won't remember it anyway.
- **Practice.** Give the talk to colleagues or family members before you deliver it, and iron out the kinks.

These are the basic guidelines that will ensure an effective presentation.

LEARN THE PRESENTATION SKILL SETS

No matter what type of talk you give, there are three skill sets that you should always use. Together they will enable you to become a powerful speaker. These skill sets, known as the "three Vs," are verbal, visual, and vocal.

PERFECT YOUR VERBAL SKILLS

Most of our time in preparing for a talk is spent perfecting our verbal skills. These include

Developing a clear message for the presentation.

Making the presentation relevant to the audience.

Analyzing your listeners.

Outlining the main ideas.

Gathering evidence to support your ideas.

Organizing your information.

Creating visual aids to present verbal information.

Involving the listeners with open-ended questions.

Holding a question-and-answer session.

Your organization of the material makes the information easier to understand and more persuasive.

ADVANCE YOUR VISUAL SKILLS

Visual skills do not refer to visual aids. Visual skills are the visual images that you create as a speaker. The more interesting you are to watch, the more likely the audience is to pay attention throughout your entire presentation. Visual skills include

Making eye contact to connect with each of your listeners.

Using gestures to describe and emphasize ideas.

Using facial expressions to communicate your feelings and attitudes.

Often these skills are not incorporated and their absence can make the presentation much less interesting than it should be.

DEVELOP YOUR VOCAL SKILLS

Your voice is a key part of your tool kit as a presenter. Vocal skills include

Raising and lowering your voice level for emphasis.

Changing your pacing to stimulate the interest of your listeners.

Using pauses to make important points.

Your success as a speaker will be determined by how well you use all of these skills to make a powerful impact on your listeners.

THE 30-SECOND RECAP

In this lesson you learned how to make public speaking a more positive experience. You've gained perspective on the importance of giving business presentations, and you've been introduced to the skill sets that will make you a better speaker.

LESSON 2

Define the Central Message

In this lesson you learn how to develop the central message of a presentation and at what point to deliver it most effectively.

A humorous cartoon depicts a man thrashing around in the middle of a large pond. On the shore sits a dog watching its master. The man calls out: "Fido, get help!" The second panel of the cartoon shows the dog in a veterinarian's office being examined by the doctor. Clearly the animal had misunderstood its master's message.

How often does the same type of thing occur during a presentation? The speaker walks to the podium and begins talking. He or she presents a long series of colorful slides, filled with statistics, pie charts, and complex graphs. You try to follow along in the package of handouts distributed at the start of the presentation. While the information is interesting, the sheer quantity of it seems overwhelming. About halfway through the talk, your mind begins to wander and you start thinking about that partially finished project that's still sitting on your desk back in the office. Finally the speaker concludes and thanks the audience.

As the speaker leaves the podium, you ask yourself: What point was he or she trying to make? Perhaps it was buried somewhere in all the data and you just missed it. Sometimes the speaker's point isn't clear or easy to spot, but far more often, the speaker never really makes a point at all.

DEVELOP THE CENTRAL MESSAGE

The *central message* is part of your verbal skill set. Developing this message is the most important step in creating a successful presentation. Without a message, a presentation simply doesn't hang together. With a message, the entire presentation is like a great piece of music: All the notes fit harmoniously together around a central theme.

PLAIN ENGLISH

The **central message** is the main point of your presentation. All the information you present should add up to one simple central message.

FOCUS ON THE SUBSTANCE

Studies show that a few days after attending a presentation, most of us remember only about 5 percent of what we've heard. It's not surprising. With all the information we receive in a week, it's a wonder that any of it really sticks with us. Information is constantly being thrown at us in meetings, company reports, magazine and newspaper articles, television and radio programs, and on the Internet. Sometimes it's hard to remember what you read yesterday, to say nothing of last week or last month.

Make sure you consider this whenever you prepare a presentation. If your listeners are only going to remember 5 percent of what you tell them, you want to be certain that it includes your central message. It is the core of your presentation. Everything else is just supporting data.

The central message should be clear and simple. No one in the audience should come away having missed it.

HIGHLIGHT YOUR CENTRAL MESSAGE

It's important not to confuse your central message with the subject of your presentation. The subject is usually a large circle of information.

An example of a subject might be improving customer service in your department. That's a large subject, and there are many things you might talk about during your presentation. Your job is to focus on a single point within that subject; call it a point of light in the circle if you like. That point is your central message. It's what you want to say about the wide subject of improving customer service.

For example, your central message might be: We need to hire three more customer service representatives; or, we need to streamline our database so we have more information about each of our customers; or, we need to answer each customer's call by the second ring.

Of course, delivering a central message usually requires that you take a position and even stick your neck out. But that's often what it means to be a successful speaker.

Try this exercise. Select two of the following subjects and develop a central message around each of them.

- Your organization's niche in the marketplace
- The company's earnings in the most recent quarter
- Your organization's Web site
- The current method of giving performance evaluations
- An on-site day care center for employees
- The amount of rework in the manufacturing area
- Flextime in your department
- The speed of your organization's R&D process
- The quality of the written communications via e-mail
- Your organization's recruitment programs on college campuses

You should now have a clear sense of how to frame the central message in the subject.

INTERPRET YOUR MESSAGE'S SUPPORTING DATA

So many speakers seem to believe that their mission is to tell you everything they know about their topic. What they're giving you is nothing more than a data dump. As effective speakers, we owe our listeners much more. Our responsibility is to analyze that data, interpret what it means, explain what all of it adds up to. That's our central message.

CAUTION

Don't make your presentation a data dump. Include only information that relates to your central message, and tie the information to the message throughout your talk.

PRESENT YOUR CENTRAL MESSAGE

Good leaders are not expected to mire themselves in detail. We want them to make sense of those details for us. Great speakers present a vision. Just recall John F. Kennedy's inaugural address or Martin Luther King Jr.'s *I Have a Dream* speech.

As a speaker you're supposed to present your vision—your central message: how you see the facts, what they mean, your opinion about them, and your position on what action should be taken on them. To present your vision, or the central message of your presentation, is to lead your listeners to take the action or follow in the direction you propose.

CONSTRUCT A ONE-SENTENCE CENTRAL MESSAGE

Developing your central message is critically important. Too many speakers simply gather information, quickly create some visual aids, then stand up and deliver their presentation. They never ask themselves: How does all this information fit together? What does it all mean? What do I want my listeners to get out of it?

TIP

> For each minute that you intend to speak, spend 5 to 10 minutes planning and preparing your presentation.

If you're asked to make an impromptu presentation about developments in your work unit to a group of visiting customers, you won't have much time to prepare. When you do have advance notice, however, and you're free to select the subject yourself, deciding what to talk about should be your first step.

For example, you may be slated months in advance to speak at the local Rotary Club about an important issue that is currently confronting your organization. Start thinking about your central message. What point are you going to make? If the listeners are only going to remember 5 percent of your presentation, what do you want to make sure they remember?

When you have very little time to prepare a presentation, this type of planning is even more important. The central message becomes an organizing principle that allows you to quickly select information that relates to your message and forget everything else. Leave that material for another talk and another central message.

Once you've decided on a central message, you may want to write it down in a single sentence or two. This way you won't forget it. Even more important, you can constantly refer to this sentence as you collect information to present in your talk. All this information should relate to the central message. If it doesn't, leave it out.

CAUTION

> Keep it short. If the central message is longer than a sentence or two, then it's too long. Look at it again. You should be able to compress your main point into a few well-chosen words. These may be the same words you use to present your message to the audience.

PRESENT A SINGLE CENTRAL MESSAGE

Speakers often wonder whether a lengthy presentation should have more than a single central message. Typically your audience will find the talk confusing. Listeners expect you to make a single point and deliver it in as few words as possible. All your other ideas should be subordinate to the central message and provide support for it.

Most speakers say too much. In a presentation, shorter is generally better. No one will criticize you for keeping the talk short. Very few speakers have ever been so good that the audience wants them to keep talking. They'll thank you for getting to the point and sitting down.

BEGIN WITH THE CENTRAL MESSAGE

A human resources manager once told me that he liked to "load the cannon." I asked him what he meant by that phrase. The manager explained that he preferred to start by giving his audience a lot of background information and supporting evidence. Once they had digested it, he would make his main point. He called that loading the cannon with data, then firing it—delivering his message.

Engineers and other technical people often present information the same way, and the approach may work well in technical and academic settings, but not in the business world. By the time you "fire the cannon," the audience may already be tuned out and not hear the main point of your presentation.

Suppose you're taking a trip. You pack your bags and load them in the car. Your family jumps in the car with you and you head off down the street. But you don't tell them where you're going. "It's a surprise," you laugh. "You'll find out when we arrive." Most families would want you to stop the car right there. They'd demand to know their destination.

It's the same when you give a presentation. Your audience wants to know the point of the whole thing, where you're taking them. Otherwise they won't be able to follow your talk, nor will they want to.

TIP

> Get to the point. Giving a presentation is not the
> same as writing a mystery story. Listeners don't want
> you to save the most important information until the
> end. They want you to get to the point sooner
> rather than later.

All the preliminary evidence or supporting material won't make any
sense unless they know why you're delivering it. Tell them your central message, and then you can tell them everything else.

Make Your Point—Fast

If you bury the central message in the body of your presentation or
save it until the end, the audience won't wait for you to get to it.
They'll start growing restless, drift off into daydreams, and even fall
asleep.

One speaker, the supervisor of a manufacturing cell in a large engine
plant, made exactly this mistake when she gave her presentation. She
began by giving her audience some background information about the
cell. She explained how it had grown in staff and productivity since
she had joined the company 10 years earlier.

Then she went on to describe the current functions of the cell. The
supervisor discussed the amount of overtime that her team was putting
in each week. She mentioned the productivity awards the cell had won
in the past.

The speaker pointed out that customer complaints about the cell's
products had been increasing recently, and this problem had to be
solved as soon as possible. At the end of her talk she finally presented
her central message: The cell needed more people to do its job effectively.

Unfortunately, long before she reached her central message, the audience had lost interest in what the supervisor was saying. They had no

idea why she'd presented all the preliminary information, what point she was trying to make, or what she wanted them to do.

Present the central message at the beginning of your presentation with sentences like these:

- The main point I want to make today is …

- The one thing I want to emphasize is …

- My central message is …

- My purpose in speaking to you is …

Only if you give your listeners a clear direction of your presentation at the outset can you hope to have them with you at the end.

GET YOUR CENTRAL MESSAGE ACROSS

Every successful central message has several key attributes. It should be

- Simple.

- Short.

- Clear.

- Delivered at the beginning.

The central message is crucial; don't be afraid to repeat it several times during the presentation.

THE 30-SECOND RECAP

In this lesson you learned how to develop a central message and when to deliver it so that it will provide structure for your presentation.

LESSON 3
Know Your Listeners

In this lesson you learn about the importance of the audience and how to perform a listener analysis so you can make your presentations more effective.

Every business presentation involves a speaker and at least one listener, if not an entire group of them. This seems pretty obvious. But you'd be surprised at how many speakers seem to operate as if their audience didn't exist. They stare at the floor, speak in a boring monotone, and show very little passion for what they're saying. Not surprisingly, their presentations usually fall on tuned-out ears.

Effective speakers don't speak to thin air; they speak to their listeners.

REMEMBER WHOM YOU'RE SPEAKING TO

Most of us probably don't look forward to preparing a business presentation. It's easy to become completely absorbed in the process of gathering information, preparing visual aids, and creating handouts. As a result, you may forget about the most important issue of all: What does your audience want to know?

This problem becomes especially noticeable when a speaker introduces a new policy or procedure. Generally the information is presented from the speaker's point of view, not the listeners'.

 TIP

> Remember the audience. The most important person in any presentation is not the speaker, but the listener.

A speaker I recall began by describing a new quality management program that he and his team had developed and explaining what the new program would accomplish. This was his central message, and, quite rightly, he introduced it at the beginning of the talk.

Then he gave a long background description of each step that his team had taken to decide on the elements of the new program. While this information may have been interesting to him, since he was involved in the process, it held little or no interest for his listeners. What they wanted to find out was how the new program would impact their jobs.

But the speaker did not introduce this information. Instead, he contrasted the new program with the old way of doing things. He pointed out that the quality of the company's products had been suffering in the past. Since many of his listeners believed that they had been doing a quality job, they found his words highly insulting.

Finally the speaker tried to explain the advantages of the new process and how it would impact the listeners. This is what they had been waiting to hear. But it came far too late in the talk—after the audience had been told they were not doing quality work. The result was that most of the listeners were so upset that they had already stopped paying attention by the time the speaker made his point.

The speaker had violated a cardinal rule of good presentations: Always put yourself in the shoes of the listeners and give them the type of talk you would want to hear. Ask yourself how your words would sound to you if you were listening to them. Then decide what you're going to say and how you'll say it.

GIVE THEM THE MEANING

Perhaps you're familiar with the acronym WIIFM. It stands for "What's in it for me?" That's the key question on the minds of your audience as they sit down to listen to your central message. They want to know

- How will it benefit me?

- How can I use this information in my job?

- Why is the central message relevant to my life?

- What does it mean to my future here?

- What is the impact of the message on how I do my job?

Another way to describe WIIFM is the *meaning of the message,* which you can find out more about in the section in this lesson called "Begin with the WIIFM."

PLAIN ENGLISH

The **meaning of the message** is how the central message relates to the listeners and what they're likely to get out of it.

MAKE THE MESSAGE MEANINGFUL

As part of the planning stage for every presentation, you should begin by developing a central message. (see Lesson 2, "Define the Central Message"). After that, determine a second element that describes the meaning of your message to the listeners.

Practice this by doing the following exercise:

1. Decide who your audience will be for a presentation.

2. Select two of the following topics and write a central message for each.

3. Write an additional sentence to express the meaning of the message for your listeners.

The sample topics are

- Cycle time on the manufacturing floor.

- Moving allowances for transferred employees.

- Employee participation in community service projects.

- Better safety programs at your plant.

- Improving tuition assistance programs.

- E-marketing on the company Web site.

- Sabbatical leaves for managers.

You're ready to decide when in your presentation you should state the meaning of the central message.

BEGIN WITH THE WIIFM

When should you introduce the WIIFM, or the meaning of the message, in your presentation? At the beginning, along with the central message. Listeners want to know what's in it for them as soon as possible. It's the best way to ensure that they'll pay attention for the rest of the talk.

CAUTION

Don't keep the audience in suspense. Always look at your talk from the listeners' perspective. They want to know what's in it for them. You should deliver this information just before your central message or just after it.

To introduce the meaning of the message, you might use sentences like these:

- This is how the (central message) will affect you. As of next Monday ...

- How would you like to make your job easier and more interesting?

- These are the ways this will benefit you.

This may sound like an unsubtle way to introduce the meaning of the message, but your audience will rarely criticize you for being too clear or too straightforward. Communicate the meaning of the message as directly as possible. Next to the central message, it is the most important part of your presentation. Indeed, a statement about the message's benefits may be even more important than the message itself: It may persuade the audience to support your vision.

TIP

> Give your WIIFM statement impact. Make the meaning of your message as powerful as possible. Remember: The audience will only listen if they think your message relates to them.

UNDERSTAND YOUR LISTENERS' PRIORITIES

Since the listeners are the most significant people in any business presentation, you should try to know as much about them as possible. This will enable you to present your information in a way that is most likely to appeal to them and hold their interest.

How do you find out about the characteristics of your listeners? Many talks are given to internal audiences, so you may already know many of the key players. If not, talk to colleagues in the organization who may know them. Find out what they are expecting from your presentation.

Preparing a speech for an external audience can be more difficult. Your listeners may be potential customers, employees in another company that is merging with yours, a civic group, or a professional organization. In that case, you may need to: look for material about your audience in business publications or on the Internet; network to key people in the organization; or, if you've been asked to address a civic group, get as much information as possible from the person who invited you about the group and what they're expecting.

RESEARCH AUDIENCE ATTITUDES

The material you gather about your audience should be aimed at answering some key questions.

Are they in your corner, against you, or straddling the fence? This information is critical if you're trying to persuade them to adopt your point of view. You'll need to work a lot harder if most of the audience doesn't see things the way you do.

CAUTION

Make sure you get off on the right foot, by describing any benefits that the audience might derive from supporting your position. If your message is about new procedures, frame your criticism of the current system carefully to avoid offending people who produced the work.

If the key players are resistant, what would convince them to support you? Sometimes you can find out the main reasons why some of the key players in your audience might not support you. It may help to structure your entire talk around dealing with their objections.

How much does the audience know about your topic? Many speakers must address audiences where there are different levels of knowledge and sophistication on a subject. Always pitch your presentation to the lowest common denominator.

What are their positions in the organization? Clearly you would give a different type of talk to peers or subordinates than you would deliver to a meeting of the board of directors of your company.

How do they like their information presented? Some people are persuaded by numbers. They like pie charts and line graphs. Others remember anecdotes or a speaker's personal experiences. The best approach is to vary the way you present information. In a mixed audience, there should be something for everyone.

How long do they expect you to speak? Find out how much time you'll be given. This will enable you to plan the presentation. No one likes a speaker who runs on too long. On the other hand, if the program planner has given you 20 minutes, she wants to make sure you fill the time slot so she's not left with an embarrassing hole in the schedule.

What are they likely to wear? You should always dress appropriately for the occasion. Don't show up in business casual attire if the entire audience is wearing suits. A good rule of thumb is to dress one level above your audience. For example, if they're wearing work clothes, you should be dressed in business casual. That way, you won't feel awkward but you'll still stand out from the audience, as befits a speaker.

DETERMINE YOUR GOAL

As you plan a presentation and think about your audience, ask yourself: What do I want them to do as a result of my presentation? In short, what is your goal? Speakers who fail to ask themselves this question fall far short of achieving their goal.

Perhaps your goal is simply to deliver information to your listeners. You may be giving them a progress report on the installation of a new computer system or you may want them to know about the benefits of a new employee assistance program.

Your goal could be more ambitious. You want to explain a new procedure, step by step, so your listeners will be able to carry it out. It may involve something as simple as the action to be taken in case of a fire drill. Or it may involve something more complex, like the standard procedure for writing technical reports.

Sometimes your goal may be to entertain an audience. If you're speaking at a roast or a retirement dinner, for example, your talk would remain light and humorous.

The most ambitious goal of all is to persuade, or to convince an audience to take action. You may want the listeners to fund a new research project. Getting a key decision-maker to write a check can be difficult because the money might just as easily be spent on something else. You must plan your talk carefully and deliver it forcefully to achieve such ambitious goals.

CONTINUALLY MEASURE YOUR PRESENTATION'S EFFECTIVENESS

Whatever your goal may be, you can tell whether you're achieving it by examining the faces of your listeners. As you look out at each one of them

- Do they seem to understand what you're saying? Or do they look confused?

- Are they paying attention? Or do they seem to be daydreaming or slipping off to sleep?

- Are they nodding in agreement? Or are they shaking their heads as you make your key points?

Whether you realize it or not, each of us is a salesperson as we stand up in front of a group and make a presentation. We must present our information or deliver our explanations in a way that will make them credible and believable to the audience. We must present our persuasive arguments so convincingly that the audience will take action on them.

As good speakers, we're in the business of making a significant impact on our listeners. And we measure success one listener at a time.

THE 30-SECOND RECAP

In this lesson you learned the importance of delivering a talk that will appeal to your listeners' interests and priorities.

LESSON 4

Energy for Effectiveness

In this lesson you learn how to use energy to add power to your presentations.

One of my colleagues, a communications consultant, serves on the board of a local nonprofit organization. Recently he was asked to become a member of the fund-raising committee. Knowing next to nothing about fund-raising, he decided to take a course at a well-known training institute.

The program was taught by a woman widely respected in philanthropic circles because she had raised millions of dollars for charity. My colleague arrived early in the morning and took his seat along with 20 other people from various charitable agencies in the area. Many of them were new to fund-raising, and they had come to learn the latest techniques from a recognized expert.

The course was very well structured, the information based on the instructor's own fund-raising experiences. It was presented clearly, and it related directly to many of the issues my colleague was grappling with at his own organization. At first, all his attention was focused on the speaker, and he tried to learn as much as possible.

As the morning wore on, however, his concentration started to flag. He thought about a problem he was trying to solve for one of his clients. Then he thought about a suspense thriller he'd seen over the weekend.

At first the lapses in his concentration lasted only a few seconds, but gradually they became longer. At one point, he realized that the speaker had presented several important ideas and he hadn't heard any of them. In fact, he was struggling to stay awake.

Finally, the training program broke for lunch. "Perhaps the afternoon session will be more interesting," he thought. Sadly, it wasn't. About 2:30 P.M., the instructor signaled a break. My colleague decided to take advantage of the opportunity; he collected the materials that had been handed out at the beginning of the class and headed for the door—never to return.

"As I left the building," he recalled, "I tried to figure out why I didn't want to stay for the entire session. The information was clear, and I was very interested in learning more about fund-raising. Then I realized that it was the speaker. She lacked any enthusiasm for her subject. In fact, she was deadly boring!"

SPEAK WITH ENERGY

If you want to be a good speaker, it's not enough simply to present a clear central message. Nor is it sufficient for you to make the message relevant to your listeners so that they'll be interested in it.

Effective speakers do more: They bring a passion and commitment to what they're saying. This passion is infectious. It spreads to the audience and keeps them involved and excited about the speaker's topic, even through a long presentation. This excitement is called *energy*.

PLAIN ENGLISH

> **Energy** is enthusiasm and passion for your message. Energy should fill your entire delivery so the audience will more readily remain focused on you and what you have to say.

SUPPLY THE ENERGY COMPUTERS CAN'T

Computers are very versatile instruments that can deliver entire presentations, complete with magnificent visual aids. But there's at least one thing they can't do and you can: bring energy and enthusiasm to a presentation.

Unfortunately, many speakers seem to forget this fact. They spend all their time on the verbal component of a presentation—the words. Then they stand up and deliver their material in a boring monotone, with their eyes focused on the back wall instead of on the audience.

They think that words alone, as long as they're clear and 100 percent accurate, will hold the interest of the listeners.

Why not deliver the presentation via e-mail? It would have the same impact and save the speaker and the listeners a great deal of time.

TIP

> Say it with energy. One of the best ways to add value as a presenter is to use energy when you deliver a talk.

Energy makes all the difference between a boring presentation and an effective one because

- Energy is the human touch that you bring as a speaker.

- Energy gives the audience a reason for assembling and listening to you instead of reading a report about your topic.

- Energy is one of the key differences between a great speaker and a mediocre one.

- Energy will ensure that you, and your message, are remembered by the audience.

Energy involves two of the skill sets that were introduced in Lesson 2, "Define the Central Message." They are your visual skills and your vocal skills.

USE VISUAL ENERGY TO STIMULATE

Many people who take a public-speaking class for the first time recall that a teacher in school once told them not to use their hands when they speak. Gestures, they were warned, might be distracting and make them look like used-car salespeople. As a result, they stand in front of a group with their hands locked together or possibly playing with a ring.

CAUTION
Pay attention to your hands. If you find your hands are doing things that have no relation to what you're saying, stop. These gestures may only distract the listeners from your talk.

When used effectively, gestures can add a great deal of energy to your presentation.

Facial expressions are also part of your visual tool kit, but too many speakers seem content to adopt one deadpan expression throughout their entire presentation. Speakers who smile at appropriate moments, raise an eyebrow, or show some enthusiasm on their faces add immeasurably to the impact of their presentations.

REINFORCE YOUR MESSAGE WITH GESTURES

We live in a visual age. Most of us are accustomed to being stimulated by the colorful images on television, in films, and on the Internet. We expect the same things from speakers.

As a presenter, you can use gestures to create powerful visual images that reinforce the words you speak before a group. The more visually interesting you can be, the more likely you are to stimulate and hold the attention of your audience.

TIP

> Remain the focus of attention. Effective gestures help ensure that your listeners will concentrate on you throughout an entire presentation. You'll be too visually interesting for them to tune out and ignore.

The next time you deliver a presentation, try the following approach to using gestures:

1. **Face the audience and plant your feet firmly and slightly apart.** Some speakers like to pace back and forth in front of their listeners. But the pacing rapidly becomes a distraction.

2. **Start with your arms at your sides.** This should be their resting position. From this position, it's easy to raise up your arms and gesture. If you lock your hands, they tend to stay there and never come apart.

3. **As you make an important point, use one or both hands for emphasis.** Don't repeat the same motion continually or you'll rapidly become boring.

4. **When you describe something, use your hands to create a visual image.** If employment figures are going up, for example, indicate this by raising an arm. If inflation is declining, show it by lowering your arm.

5. **Make your gestures as expansive as possible.** Don't look like you're addressing an audience from a phone booth. Enlarge your gestures and extend your arms. Don't worry, you won't look like a carnival barker.

6. **Don't try to plan your gestures.** A former U.S. president was told to improve his speaking style by using gestures.

Unfortunately, they looked too planned and artificial, which only made his presentations worse. Most of us use gestures naturally in normal conversation. Apply the same principles when you stand up in front of a group.

TIP

> Become aware of the way you use gestures in conversation. Most of us are pretty animated. You need even more animation when you speak to a group because it's larger and you must stimulate more people.

7. **Move out of your comfort zone.** As you start using more gestures in a presentation, it will seem uncomfortable at first. You'll feel as if you're overdoing it. If possible, videotape yourself as you rehearse your presentation. You'll probably be surprised to discover that you weren't as animated as you thought and can use even more visual energy in your presentations.

HUMANIZE PRESENTATIONS WITH FACIAL EXPRESSIONS

Recently I was on a flight from Houston and watched a sitcom on the television monitor without putting on the headphones. It was amazing to discover how much I could figure out about the story simply by watching the characters' gestures and facial expressions, their body language was so demonstrative.

Good speakers use the same approach with their audiences. It's another way to humanize a presentation and make a connection with your listeners.

Show a human face. Look at your listeners, and don't be afraid to smile or grimace when you speak. Audiences generally like to know that there's a real person standing up there with real feelings that show up on your face.

Use Vocal Energy for Power

When you're speaking to another person, especially about a topic of great interest to you, your voice generally demonstrates that enthusiasm. However, many of us seem to believe that a different approach is necessary when we run a business meeting or deliver a formal presentation. Somehow these activities seem to call for a dry tone of voice that remains at the same level from start to finish.

Who says business presentations are supposed to be this way? If you want to ensure that your audience tunes you out, speak in a monotone. It will have the same effect as listening to soothing music designed to lull you to sleep.

A speaker I once heard had the kind of voice a hypnotist would use to put a patient in a trance. Unfortunately, when he delivered his key points, his audience was far too glassy-eyed to hear them.

CAUTION

If you're unfortunate enough to speak directly after lunch, you need to work even harder to keep your listeners awake. Don't speak in a monotone. You must use your voice to inject as much energy as possible into your talk.

To keep your audience's attention and get your message across, use these elements in your vocal skill set:

- **Loudness.** You should raise and lower the level of your voice during your presentation. Varying the level helps ensure that your audience stays awake. By raising your voice, you can also add emphasis to important points.

- **Pacing.** Changing the pacing is another way to add interest to your presentation. Speak a little faster during one section, although not so fast, of course, that the audience can't follow you. Then slow down as you get to an important point.

- **Pausing.** Many good speakers have learned how to use pauses very effectively. As they reach a key statement, they pause just before delivering it. This keeps the audience wondering what's coming next.

- **Tone.** You can communicate volumes about the words you speak by the tone of voice you use. Tone can signify approval or disdain, enthusiasm or disappointment.

Start strong, moderate your vocal energy in the body of the talk, and then end with the highest energy you can muster.

BE PASSIONATE TO BE PERSUASIVE

You can't hope to persuade your listeners to change the way they do things unless you sound convinced yourself. Energy puts passion into your presentations. The best speakers know how to combine visual and vocal energy to deliver their words.

In short, all three channels—visual, vocal, and verbal—are open and operating together in an unforgettable presentation.

THE 30-SECOND RECAP

In this lesson you learned how to use visual and vocal skills to add power to your presentations.

Lesson 5
Eye-Contact Communication

In this lesson you learn about the value of eye contact in communicating with your listeners.

Think about all the people you're likely to meet throughout your career; many more than your parents or grandparents, who may have gone to work for an organization and stayed there until retirement. Each time you start another job and meet new colleagues, the ritual is usually the same. You extend your hand, look the other person in the eye, and introduce yourself.

Perhaps you were one of those people who was told repeatedly by your parents, "Always look someone in the eye when you shake hands." It's a way of being polite, of showing respect, and it can even help you remember someone's name after you first meet.

Interact Through Eye Contact

Eye contact is part of human interaction, whether you're communicating one to one or speaking in front of a group. Studies show that we receive more than 50 percent of our information visually.

Consider what your eyes tell you about other people. You can read their body language and find out if they're feeling comfortable with you or tense and awkward. You can look into their eyes to determine whether they communicate empathy and support or cold indifference.

A major difference between e-mail and in-person communication is that your eyes can pick up subtle signals and hidden messages that e-mail will never reveal. It's one of the reasons why world leaders want to meet face to face, so they can take the measure of each other.

You can also use your eyes to make closer contact with the people in your audience. Your eyes can communicate a wide range of emotions. You can also use your eyes to focus attention on individual listeners and make them feel special and important.

In short, eye contact is part of the added value you, as a good speaker, bring to a presentation.

TIP

> Establish eye contact with your listeners from the beginning of your talk to enhance your effectiveness as a presenter.

AVOID EYE-CONTACT BLUNDERS

When it comes to making eye contact with an audience, speakers use a variety of approaches. Those you should beware of using are

- **Peekaboo.** Some speakers like to put their laptop computers on the lectern to project slides. Then they stay hidden behind the computer and deliver the entire presentation without ever making eye contact with their audience.

- **I'm too busy!** The speaker is completely preoccupied reading a prepared text or a set of notes and never looks up and acknowledges that the audience is in the room.

- **Please, help me!** These speakers spend much of the time looking up at the ceiling as if they're hoping for divine intervention to help them through their talk.

- **I'm reading the eye chart.** Similar to the last approach, except that this time the speaker is staring at the back wall as if reading an eye chart throughout the presentation.

- **I'm not worthy to stand in front of you.** These presenters keep their eyes cast down at the floor as they speak. They seem to be saying that they're unqualified to address the audience.

- **Watching a tennis match.** Some speakers try to make eye contact by *scanning* the room. Their heads are constantly moving back and forth as if they're watching a tennis match.

PLAIN ENGLISH

> **Scanning** is a method of eye contact in which the speaker's eyes are continually moving from one person to another. This approach will leave your eyes tired, your neck aching, and the audience wondering what you're trying to accomplish.

Speakers who adopt one or more of these techniques usually do so because they're nervous and afraid to look at any individuals in the audience. Unfortunately, any of the preceding approaches prevent you from making real contact, whether it's in a conversation or with your listeners. You risk having the people you're talking to feel ignored—or even worse—unappreciated and insulted.

USE THE THREE-STEP APPROACH

As you may recall from earlier lessons, eye contact is one of the techniques in your visual skill set. Used correctly, your eyes can significantly increase your impact as a speaker. Here's an approach that has proven to be quite successful:

1. **Find a pair of eyes.** As you begin your talk, look for one person in the room and speak directly to that individual.

2. **Deliver a thought.** Continue looking at that person until you have communicated a complete thought. How long is a thought? It can be an entire sentence. Or it can be much shorter—the information between the commas in a sentence. For example, suppose you were saying: "We need to expand

our sales in Europe, in Latin America, and in the Far East."
You might deliver only the opening of the sentence (the
information before the first comma) to one individual.

3. **Pause and look at someone else.** After you finish delivering
a thought to one person, pause and move your eyes to someone else. Then communicate your next thought.

CAUTION

> Keep your eyes focused on your audience. Never
> deliver a thought unless you are speaking to a pair
> of eyes.

Use this approach throughout your entire presentation. It enables you
to make person-to-person contact with individual listeners in your
audience.

You may be thinking that this technique might work with small audiences, but you couldn't possibly look at each person in an audience of
100 or more. That's true, but you don't have to look at every person
who's there. When you look at one of them and deliver a thought, the
people sitting nearby imagine that you're looking at them, too.

Remember that you're probably standing some distance away, so it's
difficult for your audience to be sure of whom, exactly, you're really
looking at.

FIND YOUR EYE-CONTACT PATTERN

As your eyes move from one listener to another, avoid a regular pattern of making eye contact. For example, if people are sitting in a U-
shape, don't start with a listener at one end and work your way from
person to person around the room. Start with a listener on one side,
then look at someone on the other side, then look at a listener in the
middle. This will prevent listeners on the far end from dozing or day-

dreaming because they figure you'll have to go around the entire room before you look at them.

It may take you some time to grow accustomed to using eye contact effectively, but if you make a conscious effort to speak to one person, pause, then speak to another, you'll reap huge benefits as a presenter.

EYE-CONTACT QUESTIONS AND ANSWERS

Here are the answers to some of the most common questions people have about eye contact:

How long should I look at a person? I don't want to stare and make the individual feel self-conscious. Use your own judgment. About 6 seconds spent looking at one person usually seems long enough. But if you have several allies in the audience and want to spend more time making eye contact with them, then do so.

Should I try to spend about the same amount of time looking at each person during a presentation? Obviously you can't time it exactly. Try not to shortchange anyone. Sometimes, people sitting in the back or on the far side of a room feel as if the speaker is paying no attention to them. Be sure you don't overlook those listeners.

How should I deal with a key decision-maker? You'll probably want to focus more eye contact on this listener because he or she has more power than anyone else. But make sure you know who the real decision-maker is. Some speakers have been fooled, and they've given too much of their attention to the wrong person.

As you've gathered, there is no fixed pattern for making eye contact, but if you practice the advice in this lesson your use of eye contact will become more effective with every presentation.

CONTROL PACING THROUGH EYE CONTACT

It may sound counterintuitive, but your eyes can actually control the pace of your presentation.

Most of us have a tendency to talk much too fast. Perhaps it's only a reflection of the speed at which events seem to move in the twenty-first century. Perhaps you also find yourself with too many job responsibilities, so you constantly feel the need to hurry through each activity.

Many speakers talk too rapidly out of nervousness and a natural desire to get the presentation over with as quickly as possible. But whatever the reason, speaking too fast can make it very difficult for an audience to follow what you're saying.

Using the proper method of eye contact can eliminate this problem. Deliver a thought to one listener, pause as you switch your eyes to another listener, then—*and only then*—deliver your next thought. This will reduce the pace of your presentation. Your audience will thank you for it.

TIP

> Since patterning eye contact is not something we naturally do when making a presentation, it will take practice. But you'll quickly discover that pausing in between thoughts will not only work wonders on your pacing, it will give you a little extra time to think about what you're going to say next.

GET FEEDBACK THROUGH EYE CONTACT

Eye contact opens an important two-way channel of communication between you and your listeners. Not only can you communicate your interest in them, they can give you critical feedback on your performance as a presenter.

Here are some of the signals to look for and what you can do in response:

- *Some listeners already have their eyelids at half-mast.* Your energy level is probably too low. Raise your visual and vocal energy.

- *Your listeners look confused after you explain a key point.* Your explanation or visual aid was probably not clear enough. Go over the information again.

- *A key decision-maker is shaking her head from side to side.* You obviously failed to convince this person. It's time to roll out a more persuasive argument.

- *Your supervisor starts reading his mail.* You're probably boring him. Maybe you can inject some information—an anecdote, for example—that will interest him. Or perhaps your talk has already gone on too long and you should bring it to a speedy close.

- *Your audience is watching you with rapt attention.* Great! Whatever you're doing is working well. Keep up the good work.

TIP

> Plan ahead. Your audience analysis should help you figure out what will and won't work with your listeners. But sometimes you can be wrong, so prepare an additional story or slide or some backup statistical data to use if you're losing your listeners.

Person-to-person eye contact is a way to get an instant evaluation from your listeners. You can read it in their eyes and in their body language. If what they're telling you is negative, you can often react quickly to put your presentation back on track.

PRACTICE YOUR NEW PRESENTATION SKILLS

So far you've been introduced to a variety of verbal, vocal, and visual skills. Clearly it's difficult to practice all of them at once. You're probably already spending enough time on the words for your presentation.

The vocal and visual skills, on the other hand, may be new to you. So you'll need to spend more time on them.

At first, using gestures, vocal energy, and eye contact may take you out of your comfort zone. It's just like trying any new skill. Concentrate on only one skill at a time and use it as much as you can in your next presentation. Then keep adding more of the skills to your repertoire as you give additional presentations. Soon you'll be using all of them successfully.

THE 30-SECOND RECAP

In this lesson you learned about using eye contact to improve your presentations.

Lesson 6
Gather Your Evidence

In this lesson you learn how to collect material to support your central message.

Where do business leaders get their information? Generally, it comes from reading great amounts of information, drawing on their own past experiences—successes as well as failures—and, perhaps most important, talking to many different people.

For example, Michael Bonsignore, chairman and chief executive of Honeywell International, spends two weeks each year traveling to the company's plants and holding town meetings with employees. For Bonsignore and leaders like him, this information becomes the raw material for their presentations. They know where to look for important, new ideas; how to organize this material logically; and how to present it persuasively to their audiences.

UNDERSTAND THE IMPORTANCE OF EVIDENCE

If every talk consisted of only a central message and the meaning of the message, it would be very short—perhaps no more than a minute or two. You may be thinking that this would be a welcome change from all those long-winded presentations that you currently suffer through every week. And you're right.

Yet without supporting *evidence,* the central message would be like a gossamer floating on air. It's simply your opinion and nothing more. Good evidence is essential because it

- Grounds your central message and gives it a structural framework.

- Logically supports your point of view.

- Confirms that you've done your homework on your topic.

- Demonstrates your expertise as an authority on the material that you're presenting.

PLAIN ENGLISH

Evidence is data that either proves or disproves a viewpoint, like the material presented in a court of law to prove a person's innocence or guilt.

Evidence is an essential element in a presentation, but before you get down to the tough business of gathering it, you'll have to do some preliminary work.

MIND-MAP YOUR MATERIAL

One of the most effective approaches to gathering evidence is a process called *mind-mapping*. Here's how it works:

1. Draw a circle in the middle of a piece of paper.

2. Inside the circle write your central message.

3. Think of ideas that will support your message. You may have gathered these from your reading or from conversations with other employees.

4. Write a brief description of each idea on a line that radiates out from the circle.

Don't discard any idea; include everything that comes to mind.

Your paper will look something like a spider's web. Now go back and examine all the ideas that are in front of you. Some may seem irrelevant or trivial and can easily be eliminated. Others may seem related to each other and can be grouped together.

Finally, you should have several important ideas that support your central message. These will become your primary pieces of evidence.

PLAIN ENGLISH

Mind-mapping is a process of brainstorming ideas related to your central message and graphically displaying them so you can decide which ones are relevant and important.

Don't regard the mind-mapping process as final. Think of yourself as an explorer. While putting together your presentation, you may uncover another key idea that should be included. Add it to your talk, like a new river being drawn on an explorer's map.

CHOOSE THREE SUPPORTING IDEAS

Presenters often wonder how many supporting ideas they should include in a presentation. Another way to look at this question is to ask yourself: How much can my listeners remember?

Perhaps you're planning to include handouts in your presentation, so you decide that it's safe to present a great amount of material because the audience can always review the handouts later. Don't kid yourself. Most people may never look at those handouts again.

It's best to operate as if the only information your listeners are likely to remember is what you say. Recall the 5 percent rule, which studies show is the amount of information that listeners will retain after a presentation. Perhaps they'll remember as many as five to seven key ideas, but more likely it'll be only about three.

There's something about the number three. All of us are familiar with the three musketeers and the three blind mice. Most presentations consist of three parts—an opening, a body, and a conclusion. Three of anything seems to be a quantity that's easy for us to remember.

TIP

Try to use the power of threes in your presentations.
Present three key ideas as supporting evidence.
Under each idea, introduce no more than three
related concepts.

PRESENT YOUR IDEAS CREATIVELY

Most of us recall ideas best when they're presented not simply as
abstract concepts but in a form that we can see—at least in our mind's
eye. In literature, among the most popular devices are metaphors and
similes. An author will take an abstract emotion like fear and describe
it as a "gnawing at the pit of the stomach," for example. That gives
readers a way to relate to the idea of fear.

You can do the same thing as a speaker: Dress up your ideas in bright
clothes and present them in interesting ways to bring them to life for
your listeners. Here are a few ways to do it:

- **Analogies.** These are like metaphors and similes, which suggest comparable qualities of things. For example, a speaker
  might compare the current structure in his organization to a
  patchwork quilt without any clear design. Another speaker
  might make a comparison between the company's manufacturing process and a smooth-running automobile. Analogies
  help listeners to visualize what the speaker is talking about.

- **Statistics.** Many business presentations are filled with
  statistics—sometimes to the exclusion of everything else.
  Obviously statistics are appropriate if you're delivering a
  financial report to the CEO, but they can be overdone with
  other audiences that may not think in statistical terms.

- **Quotations.** Quotes from a recognized expert in a field can
  lend the voice of authority to what you're saying. They can
  come from articles in magazines and newspapers, and many
  publications also host online forums where you can find out

what other people are thinking about your topic. In addition, some speakers like to use quotations from their peers, subordinates, or customers to give credence to a central message.

- **Examples.** These can come from almost anywhere. Perhaps you've used examples from other companies in your field to provide support for your key points. You might also draw examples from vendors and customers. Each time you can cite a "for instance" it strengthens your arguments.

TIP

Variety broadens the appeal of your material. Some listeners relate best to statistics, while others may prefer analogies or anecdotes.

- **Anecdotes.** Personal stories from your own experience or from someone else's seem to be retained by many listeners long after a presentation has ended. Introduce a concept, then follow it with an anecdote to illustrate your point. Or tell your story, then draw a moral or a point from it. Either approach can be extremely effective.

Try to include as much variety as possible in the way you present your ideas. Variety is one way to keep your audience interested and involved in your presentation.

PLAN YOUR INFORMATION-GATHERING PROCESS

Collecting information for your presentation may stretch out over several days or several weeks, depending on when you start working on a scheduled speech. Make sure you leave enough time to do an adequate job.

As you come across articles or other data that look promising, store them away in a file. You'll probably collect far more than you need.

But this will give you a broad range of material from which to make your final selections.

Draw from your own experiences. Before you start collecting data, don't forget to mine your own experiences for possible quotations, anecdotes, and so on. Spend some quiet time thinking about things you know that could support your ideas, and expect some useful thoughts to occur to you while you're taking a shower, jogging, or commuting to work.

APPLY CRITERIA FOR INCLUDING EVIDENCE

Since you'll probably have more information than you need, how should you decide what to include and what to omit? Use the five-C test:

- **Correct.** The material must be accurate. You don't want to present anything that has flaws in it. This will only be an embarrassment.

- **Complete.** Make sure that the information, especially statistical data, is complete, and there are not any important points missing.

CAUTION

Don't take any chances with your evidence. All of it should conform to the five-C criteria. Otherwise, you may risk undermining the strength of your arguments and losing your audience.

- **Clear.** An analogy or anecdote should be easy to understand and clearly relate to your central message or supporting evidence.

- **Consistent.** The evidence you present should be consistent with the expectations of your audience. One speaker I recall opened her presentation with an off-color joke that seemed completely inappropriate to the occasion. The audience was turned off for the rest of her talk.

- **Clever.** Try to select examples that will stimulate your audience, not boring, overused material.

Once you've gathered information, you're ready to take a first stab at an outline for your presentation.

CREATE A PRELIMINARY OUTLINE

You now have the ideas and the supporting evidence to create a preliminary outline.

1. Write out each of your main points.

2. Under each point, list the supporting information that you have collected.

3. Evaluate the material in terms of the five criteria described in the preceding section.

4. Decide whether any point appears to be weakly supported and needs more data. If so, go back to your file and look for more information. If none is there, you may have to do additional research. Company publications may be helpful, especially if you're speaking to a group of employees about an internal problem.

TIP

> Most presentations have very tight deadlines so there usually isn't much time to find more research material if you need it. The quickest approach is the Internet. Use one of the search engines, type in your topic, and see what comes up.

The best presentations include enough evidence to convince even the most skeptical listeners.

THE 30-SECOND RECAP

In this lesson you learned how to collect, sift, and organize supporting evidence for the ideas in your presentation.

LESSON 7
Organize Your Material

In this lesson you learn how to present information in six organizing patterns so your listeners can remember it more easily.

According to a recent business survey, more and more chief information officers—the people in charge of the computers—are being promoted by their companies to CEOs. If we ever needed further proof that information is the most valuable resource an organization can possess, this is surely it.

As speakers, we operate like chief information officers, taking raw data and turning it into useful information that our listeners can use. This process involves organizing our data into points which form patterns.

LEARN THE SIX ORGANIZING PATTERNS

By creating patterns, we give shape to the data we use to support our central message. It's the same as taking the pieces of a jigsaw puzzle and fitting them together to form a picture. We enable our listeners to see that picture; that is, we bring them to a conclusion (our central message) based on the information that we present.

TIP

Develop a pattern. The pattern is like a formal outline for a talk. It will not only help you arrange your facts and points in a logical order, it will also help you remember all of them when you deliver your presentation.

The material that you deliver in a presentation can generally be organized into six different patterns. Each of them presents information in a clear, logical way.

The six patterns of organization are

- The whole and its parts.
- Chronological order.
- Problem-solution.
- Spatial order.
- The news reporter approach.
- The best alternative.

One pattern will probably work better than the others in organizing your facts for the presentation. However, you might also decide to use more than one pattern to organize different parts of the same talk.

THE WHOLE AND ITS PARTS

This is probably the most common type of pattern and the simplest one to execute. You present your central message, then break it into individual subtopics, or points, and discuss each of them.

Central Message: New, young managers are not remaining with our company for more than a year. There seem to be three reasons for this problem.

Points:

Eighty-hour work weeks

Too much travel

Compensation packages that are smaller than those our competitors offer

CAUTION

Lead with your best shot. In the whole-and-its-parts pattern, don't leave your most important point until last. Always present it first. In case any of your listeners need to leave before you finish, or lose interest in your talk partway through, at least they've heard your most important argument.

Central Message: We need to improve our tuition assistance program for employees.

Points:

> Companies need a highly trained work force to be competitive in the marketplace.

> A good tuition assistance program encourages employees to broaden their skills so they can do more than one job, making them far more valuable to our organization.

> A generous program will enable us to retain more employees.

> An effective program will enhance the reputation of our organization, attracting a higher number of talented young people.

CHRONOLOGICAL ORDER

Speakers often use this pattern to describe a series of past events that have led up to or caused a current situation. The events follow each other in a specific chronological order. In your presentation, you'd often use time order words: *first, then, next; in 1998, in 2000; in the first quarter, in the second quarter,* and so on.

Central Message: Our current manufacturing problems have resulted from a series of events that began more than two years ago.

Points:

> First we took on a large new contract without enough employees to carry it out.

> Then our vice president for quality left for another organization and was never replaced.

> Next we put too much emphasis on meeting production quotas instead of manufacturing quality products.

> Finally our major customer left us for another vendor.

Speakers also use the chronological pattern to describe the steps in a process. These steps must be presented in a specific sequence or the process will not work correctly.

TIP

> Fill in with details. These patterns provide the basic structure for a presentation. Under each subtopic, or point, you can add as many details as necessary to fully explain it.

Central Message: In case of a serious chemical spill, you must follow these steps:

Points:

> Evacuate the area upwind of the spill.
>
> Put on the proper personal protective gear.
>
> Return to the spill area and begin cleaning up the chemical.
>
> Put all cleanup materials in an approved receptacle.
>
> Hose down the area to remove any remaining chemical.

PROBLEM-SOLUTION

This type of speech usually contains three parts: a description of the problem and its impact on your organization, a discussion of the causes that created the problem, and a presentation of your solution.

Central Message: There have been too many accidents on the manufacturing floor during the past year, and we must do something to deal with the problem immediately.

Points:

> Several types of accidents have occurred: falls from ladders, burns, severe electrical shocks.

Causes include

> Inadequate knowledge of safety procedures
>
> Lack of proper training
>
> Safety procedures given too low a priority in the plant

Solutions:

> A new safety training program
>
> Regular presentations by the plant manager and his staff emphasizing the importance of safety

Central Message: Our organization must bring products to market much more rapidly.

Point:

> The problem is causing us to lose market share to our competitors.

Causes include

> A culture that has been research driven, not market driven
>
> Past dominance in our field with very little competition
>
> An unwillingness to learn from our competitors

Solutions:

> Streamlining the R&D process
>
> Benchmarking our competitors
>
> Creating teams that include research and marketing people

SPATIAL ORDER

This pattern works well when you're trying to create a visual picture for listeners. Suppose you want to explain the layout of a new facility, or the geographical distribution of your company's retail outlets. This information can be easily organized into a spatial pattern.

 TIP

> When you use a spatial order pattern, your talk will probably include various signal words, such as: *front, back, center, left, right; north, south, east, west;* or specific geographic locations such as: Atlanta, Houston, and so on.

Central Message: We're adding more stores in the South in response to increased customer demand for our products.

Points:

> Building plans for the Atlanta region
>
> Acquisition plans for existing store chain in Tampa area
>
> Construction of new stores in Charlotte region
>
> New store openings in greater Houston

THE NEWS REPORTER APPROACH

In this organizational pattern, a speaker provides answers to the five Ws: *who, what, when, where, why*, and sometimes *how*. This pattern will seem very familiar to your listeners because they read newspaper and magazine articles and watch news reports on television.

The *what* is often contained in the central message, and the rest of the presentation tries to answer the other questions.

Central Message: There is too much downtime because of smoking breaks.

Points:

> *Who:* Employees from every department are leaving their desks to smoke a cigarette.
>
> *When:* These breaks are occurring at regular intervals throughout the day, more of them for people with a heavy cigarette-smoking habit.
>
> *Where:* The smokers are congregating outside the building. Some of them must travel five floors to the smoking area. This extends their downtime.
>
> *Why:* This is an important issue because we are losing too much productivity and something must be done about it.

TIP

> Following this presentation, you might then open the meeting to a discussion about the issue and possible solutions.

Central Message: We should hold a company-wide event to celebrate our substantial sales increases in the past quarter.

Points:

When: The event could be held next Friday.

Where: The company cafeteria would provide food and drinks.

Who: All employees would be invited. But the event would recognize those teams that contributed to our increased sales.

Why: A recognition event sends all employees the message that increased sales have a very high priority in our company.

THE BEST ALTERNATIVE

This is similar to the problem-solution pattern discussed earlier. The speaker presents a problem, then considers several solutions. Each one is eliminated, in turn, until only a single, best solution remains.

Central Message: We need to improve the quality of materials that we are receiving from several of our vendors.

Points: So far we've tried various approaches to improve vendor quality:

Letters to the vendors asking them to make improvements

Visits by our CEO and her staff to vendor plants

Quality training programs for vendors sponsored and paid for by our organization

None of these approaches has been completely successful. Quality problems still exist.

Best alternatives:

> Call in vendors and threaten to end their relationship with us.

> Set a three-month time limit for them to make improvements that meet all our quality standards.

> If standards are not met, cancel our arrangements with the vendors.

WARM UP TO PATTERN-MIXING

Don't worry if one of the patterns doesn't seem to fit your presentation. It may organize itself into several of them. Or your material may be best organized as simply a series of related topics. These should be presented in order of importance, from most important to least important.

THE 30-SECOND RECAP

In this lesson you learned about six methods of organizing information for your presentation.

LESSON 8

Create Successful Presentations

In this lesson you learn how to develop an effective opening, body, and close for your presentation.

If your opening sentences are delivered in a dull monotone and they're dry as dust, the audience may decide that this is just another boring talk and they can think about something else. Hook the audience in your opening, and you can hold them in rapt attention through your entire presentation.

Listeners should not be required to work hard to figure out what you're talking about. Ease your audience through the transition from the opening to the body of your presentation by summarizing points made in the opening and sketching the outline of the body.

Your presentation shouldn't just end; close with a call to action and a specific follow-up agenda: "I'd like you to get back to me with your comments on my proposal by next Wednesday," or if you're making a financial request, direct it to the key decision-maker: "Can I look for your approval by the end of the week?"

Every good presentation should be tightly structured. It should take listeners on a straight path from the opening, through the body, to the conclusion and a call for action. Follow the advice in this lesson and you'll have the keys to a successful presentation.

OPEN WITH A FLOURISH

There's an old saying that "first impressions are lasting impressions." Your listeners form an impression of you immediately, from the first words that you speak. If you start with a high level of energy and your ideas are interesting, you're likely to have the listeners' attention.

TIP

> The most important part of any presentation is the first 60 seconds. If you don't capture the attention of your listeners then, they may decide to tune out for the rest of your talk.

It may sound pretty harsh to suggest that a presentation can be made or broken in the opening. After all, you might have spent several days putting together a 30-minute talk, designing visual aids, and printing handouts.

Unfortunately, the listeners probably don't care about all your hard work. If they aren't hooked in the opening minute, they may not hear much of what you're going to say afterward, and all your hard work will be for nothing.

Listeners are much like surfers on the Internet, clicking on and off Web sites. An audience can click you on and off just as easily. One manager explained that when he went to meetings, some of the attendees would routinely begin reading their mail a few minutes after the speaker started talking. They had already lost interest. You certainly don't want the same thing to happen when you stand up to talk.

CONSIDER FIVE SUCCESSFUL OPENINGS

There are several effective ways to open a presentation. The approach that you decide to use will depend on a couple of things:

- **Your listener analysis:** What will work best with your audience.

- **Your material:** What seems most appropriate for the information you're presenting.

OPENING ONE: CENTRAL MESSAGE AND MEANING

Every presentation should have the central message and the meaning of the message in the opening. Sometimes this is all the opening needs, especially if the central message comes as a surprise to your audience.

Suppose you were speaking to a group of Wall Street analysts who were expecting fourth-quarter earnings at your company to be down. Instead you told them that earnings were up by 5 percent. That's a startling central message that will certainly grab their attention.

CAUTION

Don't be like speakers who spend their time preparing the details of their talks and forget about the opening. Remember that every good talk must be listener-centered. Your listeners want an opening that will knock their socks off.

The meaning of the message can also be quite an attention-getter. This is where the audience finds out WIIFM (what's in it for me?—see Lesson 3, "Know Your Listeners," for more on WIIFM). If the benefits are substantial—for example, an increase in pay, more stock options, shorter work hours—your audience is sure to listen to everything you tell them.

OPENING TWO: AN ANALOGY

Some presenters like to begin their talks with an analogy. Analogies can be valuable in relating a theoretical concept to something that's familiar and easily understandable to your audience.

The more unusual the analogy, the more likely your listeners are to remember it. For example, a series of books has been published over the past few years that take the leadership skills of great historical figures and apply them to the workplace.

Among these famous leaders are Attila the Hun and General Ulysses S. Grant. Since most of us might not immediately think of Attila when looking for ideas to guide a modern CEO, the analogy attracts our attention and might even persuade us to buy the book.

TIP

> If you begin your presentation with an analogy, make sure it's an appropriate one that relates to your central message. Then tie the analogy and the message together for your listeners.

OPENING THREE: VOICE OF AUTHORITY

Another way to open a presentation is to cite an authority. This may be a quote from the president of your company, some benchmarking information from a survey you conducted of competitors in your field, or it might be some information from a newspaper or magazine article.

The more unusual and startling the information is, the greater the impact is likely to be on your listeners. Whatever material you decide to present should also be directly related to your central message.

You can present the message first, followed by the quote from the president or a statistic from the article. Or you can reverse the order and begin with the information from your authority.

Suppose you are speaking on the importance of a college education in an individual's career. You might begin with an article from *The Washington Post* that reports that seven years ago a majority of Americans believed that we had too many people with a college degree. But today 75 percent of all adults believe that we should have as many college educated young people as possible.

OPENING FOUR: TELL A STORY

Nothing is more powerful than beginning a presentation with a story that illustrates your central message. Former President Ronald Reagan was a wonderful storyteller—one of the skills that made his speeches so effective.

You can draw on a story from your own personal experience, from something you've read, or from the experiences of other people.

> ### CAUTION
> Don't be long-winded. If you plan to open your talk with a story, make it short. There's nothing worse than an anecdote that goes on and on and never seems to get to the point. The audience grows impatient and stops listening.

One of the best presentations I ever heard was delivered by a clergyman who told the story of a governor in one of the Southern states. The governor had been an orphan as a boy, and been ridiculed by children who had parents, but he worked hard, put himself through college, and eventually rose to the highest office in the state. As the governor often told other people: "I knew I was a child of God and I could do anything." This was the minister's central message.

OPENING FIVE: ARTFUL HUMOR

Speakers often wonder whether they should use a joke to open a presentation. The answer is: *It depends*—on several factors:

- **How skillful are you at telling jokes?** Some speakers forget the punch line or mix it up with the beginning of the joke, and it falls flat.

- **How well do you know your audience?** If you're going to use a joke, you must be sure that your audience will respond well to humor. Even more important, you must know what kind of humor they like. Many a speaker has told a joke that he thought was funny but the audience didn't.

CAUTION

Play it safe: Avoid off-color humor. Ribald stories are generally inappropriate for business presentations and may even offend many listeners. You'll immediately lose their support for your message.

- **How does the joke relate to your central message?**
  Speakers sometimes open with humor to break the ice, but the joke has nothing to do with their central message. Be sure there's a clear connection between your joke and the message, or the listeners may become confused and may not fully comprehend the message when it's delivered.

TRANSITION THE TALK WITH SUMMARIES

Once you've completed the introduction, segue into the body of your talk. This information should be organized according to the patterns discussed in the last lesson. Before you jump directly into the body of your talk, however, it's helpful for the listeners to know what you're planning to do.

For example, if your central message is the need for a new transportation facility, you might lead off the body of your talk by saying: "I'm going to tell you three reasons why we need to build this new facility." Then present the reasons.

After you discuss each reason, it's a good idea to briefly summarize what you said before going on to the next one. These summaries give your listeners a little breathing space, which allows them to briefly recall what you've already explained before moving on to the next point.

You might even use phrases such as, "Let me briefly review what I've covered," or, "Let's take a moment to summarize the first reason we need a new facility."

After you finish with the second reason, summarize again and briefly recall the first reason, then you can continue with words like, "the third reason we need this facility is."

Keep it simple and streamlined. If your speech becomes too complex or confusing, the listeners will probably stop paying attention.

TIP

> The structure of your presentation should be as tight as possible, with no extraneous ideas or unnecessary points. Try to relate each summary to your central message.

By telling your listeners what you plan to say and using frequent summaries, you can lead them gently to the conclusion of your presentation.

CLOSE WITH A CALL TO ACTION

The closing of your presentation is often the last opportunity you'll have to make an impact on your listeners. You want that impression to be as powerful as possible, so here are the elements to build into your close:

1. End the presentation with as much energy as possible.

2. Repeat your central message and the meaning of the message.

3. If you want your listeners to do something after leaving your presentation, make sure to give them a call to action.

Too often, meetings end without any of the participants knowing what the next step should be, or what they ought to do. As a result, meetings are often a waste of time and no action is ever taken.

The call to action, which wraps up your talk, is just what it says. You ask the listeners to do something based on what you've told them and you give them a deadline for taking action.

The 30-Second Recap

In this lesson you learned about how to develop the opening, the body, and the conclusion of a talk.

LESSON 9
Interact with Audiences

In this lesson you learn how to increase audience participation.

A children's book author was recently asked to address a group of young people and their parents on the subject of writing biography. The author decided not to deliver a lecture, which he thought would bore the audience. Instead he opened his talk with a few words about biography, then asked the children some questions. He wanted to involve them in the presentation as much as possible.

The author began by asking them what interesting biographies they had read lately. Then he wanted them to tell him why they like biographies. He also knew that some of the children were writing their own biographies about family members, so he asked them to tell him about their research.

At the end of the presentation, one of the parents came up to the author. "You know," she said, "that talk was just like having a conversation in your living room. Everybody had a chance to participate."

GET YOUR LISTENERS TALKING

Most speakers take their responsibility very seriously. Many believe that the entire burden of making a presentation should be squarely on their shoulders; in short, that they should do all the talking.

Where is it written that all the time allotted to your presentation should be filled with the sound of your own voice? Why should you put so much pressure on yourself? Wouldn't it be much easier if you could take a break from speaking and let the audience participate?

Shakespeare said that "brevity is the soul of wit." Good speakers know when to stop talking and pass the baton to members of the audience so they can become involved in the presentation.

CAUTION

Don't hog the limelight. Very few speakers are so compelling that they can fill 30 minutes or an hour completely by themselves. The audience needs a break from your voice; let them have a chance to speak. They'll thank you for it.

This turns the talk from a "you-they" to an "us" situation; all of us are involved in the presentation. The audience will be flattered at being asked for their thoughts.

AVOID THE CLOSE-ENDED QUESTION

The purpose of asking a question is to initiate a dialogue with your listeners. You want them to talk. Unfortunately, certain types of questions will elicit little or no response from your listeners. These are called *close-ended questions*. They include

- A question that can be answered with a show of hands.

  Example: How many people here enjoy public speaking?

- A question that has a yes or no answer.

  Example: Do you think the company should improve its health benefits program?

- A question that has only one correct answer.

  Example: How many sales offices do you think our organization operates in the United States?

The last question may elicit no response at all; unless people are positive of the answer they're not likely to raise their hands for fear of looking foolish.

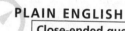

PLAIN ENGLISH

> **Close-ended questions** have only one correct answer or a brief one- or two-word response.

CREATE DIALOGUE WITH OPEN-ENDED QUESTIONS

If you want to begin a dialogue with your listeners and elicit a meaningful response from them, you must ask *open-ended questions.*

PLAIN ENGLISH

> **Open-ended questions** have no right or wrong answers or one-word responses. They ask for listeners' opinions, attitudes, feelings, and experiences.

For example, one speaker was talking to an audience about ways to expand the use of their telephones at home. This would enable them to do more work from a home office.

He discussed such things as using the phone for fax transmissions and Internet access, and adding an answering machine. After presenting his central message, the speaker asked his listeners a question:

> *How are you currently using your telephone?*

This was an open-ended question. Everyone in the audience could answer it because all of them could talk about their own experiences using the telephone. There was no right or wrong response.

Another speaker was delivering a talk on fire safety. She asked her audience this open-ended question:

> *When you hear the alarm for a fire drill, how do you respond?*

Each person in her audience had been in this situation at one time or another and could answer the question. This enabled the speaker to find out how her listeners were dealing with fire drills, which was the topic of her talk.

TIP

Dialogue questions are part of your verbal skill set. Although they may not work in every situation, you should think about using them as you prepare a talk. It's a good way of keeping your listeners involved.

INCORPORATE DIALOGUE QUESTIONS EFFECTIVELY

Have you ever attended a cocktail party and found that you didn't know a single person in the room? The feeling can be overwhelming. One way to deal with it is to walk up to someone who is standing alone, extend your hand, introduce yourself, and ask a question: "What brings you to this party?" And after you've talked about that topic, you might ask: "What kind of work do you do?"

We call these questions *ice-breakers*. Some people go so far as to make a fairly long mental list of them. If one question doesn't work, they try another.

PLAIN ENGLISH

An **ice-breaker** is a question that begins a dialogue, or interaction, between a speaker and listener(s).

One place to use a dialogue question is at the beginning of your presentation, as an ice-breaker. You can start with a question that's related to your central message, elicit a response from your listeners, then introduce the message. Or you can begin with the central message, then ask the question.

Open-ended questions can also be used almost anywhere in the body of a presentation where they seem to work.

You might even ask an open-ended question in the closing of your presentation. Then restate your central message and follow up with a call to action. This is a powerful sequence for your listeners to experience just before they leave the presentation.

PLAN AND REFINE DIALOGUE QUESTIONS

If you decide to use dialogue questions in your presentation, here are a few points to keep in mind:

- Prepare the questions carefully during the planning stage of your presentation. Think about your audience and what types of open-ended questions will work best with them.

- Remember the difference between an open-ended and a close-ended question. Sometimes you can ask a close-ended question and follow it up with an open-ended question.

  Examples: *How many people think they could be better speakers? From your own experience, what skills would make each of you a better speaker?*

- When you present an open-ended question, give your audience time to respond. Sometimes it takes that long for your listeners to realize that you've just asked them to participate in your presentation. Then they need time to formulate their response.

- If no one says anything, don't just wait a split second and immediately move on with the rest of your talk. Give the listeners time to say something.

- Sometimes an audience may be hesitant to speak. If so, respond to the question with your own experience. This will "prime the pump" and often the audience will begin talking.

TIP

The best television interviewers, people like Barbara Walters, know how to ask the right questions to get people to talk about themselves. Study their techniques to help you formulate open-ended questions.

- Remember, this is not a question-and-answer session. You don't need to respond to a listener's experience except to say something like, "Thank you," or, "That's very interesting." Then move on to someone else.

- After several people have answered the question, segue back into your presentation. At this point, it's probably a good idea to summarize what people said.

After your summary, repeat your central message, or the last key point in the body of your presentation; then introduce any new ideas.

USE DIALOGUE QUESTIONS ADVANTAGEOUSLY

One of the most important goals of every good speaker is to keep the audience awake. Once they start nodding off, everything you say is a waste of time—yours and theirs—because they won't hear it.

Dialogue questions are one way to keep your audience involved in a presentation. It's pretty hard for them to daydream if they're busy answering your questions.

A dialogue question will usually take most listeners by surprise. It's the last thing most people expect during a presentation. They were assuming that your talk would be just the same as everyone else's—that you'd do all the speaking, not them.

The element of surprise is often enough to pick up the pace of your talk. Indeed, if you see people are beginning to lose interest in what you're saying, an effective way to bring them back again is to ask a dialogue question.

TIP

Hold something in reserve. Prepare one or two extra dialogue questions just in case your talk begins to run out of gas. Audience participation is an effective way to add renewed energy to your presentation.

The primary purpose of a dialogue question is simply to involve your listeners. But sometimes a question can do even more. It can help put the audience on your side, which can be very useful, especially if you're delivering a persuasive presentation. It can also give you a better feel for the listeners' concerns, and for what they need to hear.

Suppose you're delivering a talk on expanding the usefulness of your home telephone, like the speaker in an earlier section of this chapter. You know, from your listener analysis, that most of the audience currently uses the phone for very limited purposes. Therefore, an open-ended question can open the door to your central message: Your home telephone can be far more versatile than the way it's currently being used.

One word of caution: Don't expect too much from your open-ended questions. It's enough to use them to produce audience participation.

THE 30-SECOND RECAP

In this lesson you learned how to use open-ended questions to produce a dialogue with your listeners.

LESSON 10
Visual Aids

In this lesson you learn the uses of visual aids and the fundamentals of developing effective ones.

In the past decade, speakers have relied on more and more visual aids to present their information. The first visual aid goes up to introduce the topic of their presentation and it's followed by a lengthy series of visuals, each one repeating almost word for word what the speaker is telling his audience. This is a clear case of role reversal: The overhead projector is now the presenter, and the speaker has become the aid.

Good speakers recognize that they need very few visual aids to make their key points. In fact, Louis Gerstner, the chief executive of IBM, speaks to analysts and investors every year without using any visuals. It's just Gerstner onstage, sitting on a stool, with a glass of water beside him. As one analyst commented: "It's a performance worth seeing."

Of course, visual aids can be used effectively. They can make a point better than you can make it verbally, or present complex data in a way that makes it much clearer to your audience. The key is: Less is more. Don't clutter up your presentation with visual aids just because "they're there." Use them thoughtfully and sparingly, and they will enhance your presentation.

EVALUATE YOUR VISUAL AIDS NEEDS

Developing visual aids is part of the planning stage for many presentations. Studies show that an audience remembers more when they *see and hear* something than when they only hear it. So visuals can help you get your point across. But before you decide to use them, consider the following:

Why are you using them? Visual aids should only be used when they make a point better than you can do it by yourself. Yet some speakers admit that visual aids are their crutch. They don't want to stand up and face an audience, so they let the projector do the work for them.

If you want to make sure you're *not* remembered by your listeners, turn on the projector as you begin your talk and read one slide after another. This approach is guaranteed to put your audience to sleep.

TIP

Make an impact. If you want your visual aids to make an impression, use as few as possible. With visuals, less really is more.

What do your listeners want? The audience doesn't come to look at your visuals. Frankly, you could e-mail hard copies just as easily and save them and yourself all the time a presentation takes. The listeners come to hear you. Your performance, not your visual aids, will make or break your talk.

What kinds of visuals should you create? Recently the CEO of a major manufacturing company directed his subordinates to stop using so many word slides. He was tired of looking at them. He wanted speakers to rely more on pictures—charts, diagrams, and cartoons— that could say more and deliver a message more clearly than words alone. This is really the purpose of visual aids.

How much can my visual aids tell the audience? Here again, less is always more. Too many speakers try to load their visuals with far more information than the audience can possibly absorb. Like your presentation, each visual aid should contain only one central idea, or message.

DESIGN EFFECTIVE VISUALS

Most of us have probably attended presentations where the speaker puts up a visual aid and tells us: "Now, I know you can't read this but ..." If a speaker needs to apologize for a visual, why use it in the first place? It simply detracts from the presentation.

As you design visual aids, make sure they enhance your presentation. Effective visuals have these characteristics:

- **The information is readable.** The rule of thumb is this: Project the slide onto a screen and stand in the back of the room. If you can read the information easily, then the type is large enough. Use a type size of 16 to 24 points. Also, keep the typeface simple. Usually a *sans serif* works best.

PLAIN ENGLISH

> **Sans serif** is a simple typeface that does not have little lines (serifs) projecting from the top or base of the letters. The text in this box is sans serif.

- **The colors are simple.** Desktop presentation programs like PowerPoint give you such a wide variety of colors to use in your visual aids that the choices may seem overwhelming.

  Simpler is generally better. Don't mix more than two or three colors on the same slide. It will look much too busy.

- **Stick with high contrast.** The color you select for your type or charts should contrast with the background color on your slides. Use light colors for type (such as yellow, white, and gold) with darker backgrounds (such as blue, green, and red).

- **Make your titles short.** Every slide needs a title to introduce it. But don't get carried away; a title should contain only a few words, or it's no longer a title. You may choose to use a

special color for the title that's not used in the body of the
slide so it stands out.

- **Select a design and stay with it.** Desktop presentation programs offer a variety of designs for your slides. They look so
attractive that it's easy to find yourself trying out a different
design for each slide. This simply distracts your audience.

  You don't want people focusing on the appearance of your
  visual, but on the information you present with it. Use the
  same design for every slide and keep it as simple as possible.

- **Proofread when you finish.** Carefully read your visual aids
after you complete them. There is nothing more embarrassing
than presenting a visual with a mistake in spelling, punctua-
tion, or grammar.

A computer spelling check will not pick up every spelling mistake.
For example, *there* and *their* are spelled correctly but mean different
things. If you use one incorrectly in a sentence, the spelling check
won't highlight it—unless you misspell it.

DECIDE ON TYPES OF VISUALS

Speakers commonly use several types of visuals in a presentation.
These include words, pie charts, bar graphs, line graphs, and diagrams.

WORDS

The most widely used visual aids consist of bulleted points. If you
decide to use one of these bullet slides, keep the lines short—no more
than five to eight words. It makes each line easy to read. The most
effective visuals usually contain no more than five or six lines. Otherwise the slide starts to look crowded.

CAUTION

Be sure to keep the grammatical structure consistent. On bullet slides, for instance, if the first line starts with a verb, the other lines should begin the same way.

Example:

- Make the central message clear.

- State it at the start of your talk.

- Repeat it during your presentation.

PIE CHARTS

These visual aids enable you to show the parts of a whole. Sometimes speakers try to cut the pie into too many pieces, showing 15, 20, or more parts. This is usually far too much for an audience to absorb.

Keep the pie chart simple; show only a few pieces. You might use one color for the chart, another color for type, and a third color for background to make the visual stimulating for your audience.

BAR GRAPHS

These visual devices enable you to compare several items either at a single point in time or at multiple points.

Vertical bar graphs show how several items compare with each other at various time periods. For example, you might show plant production at one facility during each month of the past year. Along the horizontal axis, you could indicate the months. On the vertical axis, you could show the units of production in thousands. Twelve bars would indicate the amount of production for every month of the year.

LINE GRAPHS

These graphs also show change over time, but as a continuous flow or line. Your graph can display the changes in one quantity, such as profits, or compare several items, such as costs of production and units sold.

Try to keep your graph as simple as possible. Don't draw in lines showing 15 or 18 different items and try to compare them. Your audience will never be able to follow what you're telling them.

DIAGRAMS

These visuals are especially valuable to show your audience a complex piece of equipment, the layout of a plant or other facility, and even the organization of your company (organization chart). A picture can truly be worth 1,000 words by showing how parts relate to each other in a way that words alone could not explain.

As with all visual aids, try to keep them as simple as possible. If you include too many labels on a piece of machinery, the audience will find the visual too complicated. Instead use several diagrams to show different parts of the machine.

USE THE POWER OF POWERPOINT

Today many desktop presentation programs enable you to create stunning visual aids on your computer. And no program is more popular than PowerPoint. This program gives your visual aids a professional look that you just can't create on your own.

With PowerPoint you can produce colorful bullet slides or design charts and graphs in far less time using one of the AutoLayouts in the program. You can also add art to your word slides by using the clip art files that come with PowerPoint. Or you can create your own drawings.

The PowerPoint program also allows you to arrange slides in one sequence, then move them around easily from place to place if you change your mind. One of the most useful parts of the program is the collection of templates. These offer a variety of different designs for your slides. Once you've selected a *template* and inserted your text and graphics, it's easy to move them around and change their dimensions.

PLAIN ENGLISH

A **template** is a master slide that creates a design and applies it to all your visuals. Templates use effective color combinations and graphics.

Some speakers also take full advantage of the transitions that Power-Point lets them create. For example, you might decide to develop a build, which means showing one piece of information on the first slide, then adding to it in successive slides until all the information is on the screen. This approach can be very effective if you only want to talk about one item at a time.

While most slides simply cut from one to the next, PowerPoint also permits you to transition by dissolving from slide to slide, which looks much smoother. In addition, you can fly in type from the right or left of the screen, or from the top and bottom. Some truly adventurous speakers also use animation to give their presentations additional sparkle.

PowerPoint visuals can be shown in a variety of formats. They can be projected as slides from your laptop computer. They can also be printed on transparencies to be displayed from an overhead projector. In addition, you can make hard copies of the visuals to hand out to your audience.

PowerPoint has become one of the most useful tools in the speaker's toolkit.

CONSIDER YOURSELF THE PRINCIPAL VISUAL

Many speakers get carried away with PowerPoint. It's easy to become so enamored of it that you forget one of the cardinal rules of presentations: *You are the most important visual.* What you create with your gestures, your facial expressions, and your eye contact are far more effective than any visual aid.

What's more, you can't cover up a lack of content with colorful visuals, no matter how many of them you use.

Recently General Henry H. Shelton, chairman of the Joint Chiefs of Staff, had to remind his subordinates to stop using so many Power-Point visuals in their presentations and get back to basics. They were packing their presentations with so many pictures of rolling tanks and animated artillery pieces that they were forgetting to present the facts. In fact a pejorative term in the military is the *PowerPoint ranger,* someone who's better at making slides than developing content. Don't let yourself fall into that trap.

THE 30-SECOND RECAP

In this lesson you learned how to use visual aids effectively in your presentations.

LESSON 11
Presenting Your Visuals

In this lesson you learn the best method of introducing your visual aids and working with them during a presentation.

Studies show that if you're trying to present new, complex information, 85 percent of the learning by your audience will occur visually, through their eyes. So visual aids can be extremely useful if you avoid cluttering your presentation with them and include only those that serve a clear purpose.

A variety of visual aids is available for speakers. In Lesson 10, "Visual Aids," we covered the process of evaluating the number and types of slides for your presentation. In this lesson we look at how to present your visuals most effectively.

MAKE YOUR VISUALS WORK

Whether you use traditional visuals such as flip charts and models, or the cutting-edge technology of PowerPoint, how you present them is key to how well they work in your presentation.

LEARN TO PRESENT TRADITIONAL VISUALS

If you handle them properly, props, models, and flip charts can be good choices, depending upon the subject of your presentation and the size of your audience.

PROPS AND MODELS

A speaker explaining the improvements in one of the parts of an air-craft engine demonstrated by holding up the old part and comparing it to the new one. After he completed his explanation, the speaker passed around the parts to his audience so they could see the improvements more closely.

Props and models are sometimes the best way of making a visual demonstration. Architects, for example, create models of new build-ings they're planning and show them to their clients to help them visu-alize how the proposed structure will look. This makes it much easier for clients to see and understand what the architects are proposing and ask questions or make suggestions at an early stage.

Props work best with small groups of listeners. A large audience would be unable to see a small engine part held up by a speaker in a large auditorium.

Props or models can be cumbersome for a speaker to carry to a pre-sentation. Nevertheless, under the right conditions, they can make an enormous impact on your audience.

 TIP

> The size of an audience often determines which visual aid will work best. Props, models, and flip charts are most effective with small groups in infor-mal settings. Slides and overheads are a better choice for larger audiences.

FLIP CHARTS

Like props, flip charts also work very effectively with smaller groups. A colleague of mine who teaches technical writing uses a flip chart extensively to put down key points in his presentation. He also uses it to write down feedback from his listeners as they critique writing sam-ples in the class.

Flip charts have several key advantages:

- They can help a speaker to interact with an audience. As you ask open-ended questions and receive important information, you can write it on the flip charts.

- They add spontaneity to a presentation. They're created on the fly in front of your listeners.

- They're flexible. The information on the chart can easily be changed and updated.

- They're colorful. If you use bold, dark colors—red, green, blue—the charts will be visually appealing.

- They can be displayed easily. Pages from the charts can be torn off and taped on the walls of a room so the audience can refer to them throughout a presentation.

 CAUTION

> Use only the top two-thirds of a flip chart. When you tear off a page and paste it on the wall, the information will be much easier for an audience to see, no matter where they're sitting.

Of course, flip charts created during a presentation may not look as professional as slides and overheads prepared in advance. But you don't need any special equipment for charts—equipment that can sometimes break down and disrupt your talk.

OVERHEADS AND SLIDES

Although the technology is now decades old, overhead projectors continue to be the most widely used audiovisual equipment in the business world. In addition to projecting overheads, a projector together with a liquid crystal display (LCD) can also display slides from your laptop computer. Other projection devices are also available for showing computer-generated slides.

There are many benefits to using slides and overheads:

- They are easy for large audiences to see.

- They give your presentation a professional look, which show-cases your knowledge and expertise to their best advantage.

- They present information in clear type and crisp colors instead of relying on the speaker's handwriting.

- Slides enable you to build in easy transitions so you can move smoothly from one visual to the next with the click of a button.

- Overheads can be flexible; if your handwriting is legible, you can create effective overheads during your talk.

Of course, overheads and slides are not without their disadvantages. These can be summed up in a single word: *equipment.* A bulb may burn out in an overhead projector, bringing your entire presentation to a complete standstill while someone searches for a replacement.

Your computer may also decide, on the day of the presentation, to develop glitches, which can stop any show dead in its tracks. Then you have to be ready to continue without the visual aids.

You should know how to deliver a powerful presentation without visuals, if necessary.

CAUTION

Don't be like some speakers, who become so depen-dent on their visual aids that they can't operate without them. If there's an equipment breakdown, they can't remember the information in their talk. Learn to deliver a presentation so you are always prepared, no matter what happens to the equip-ment.

NEVER FORGET THESE FOUR STEPS

So many speakers begin a presentation with high energy and good eye contact only to forget these essential skills when they start to present their visual aids. Somehow all their energy disappears, and instead of looking at their audience, they focus all their attention on the visual aid, talking to it with their backs to the listeners.

There is a far more effective way to work with visual aids, which enables you to continue using all your presentation skills. This process includes four steps, which are described as if you were using overheads or slides, since these are the most common visual aids.

1. **Project your first visual and walk back to the screen.** As you talk about a visual, you should always stand next to the screen. This accomplishes two things:

   a. You will not be blocking the view of anyone in the audience. If you stand next to the overhead projector or other projection device, it's easy to prevent someone from seeing the screen.

   b. By standing next to the screen, you and the visual aid present one unified image. The audience doesn't need to look back and forth to focus on the visual, and it will become the center of attention.

2. **Introduce the visual aid.** Before you talk about any of the details in the visual, give your audience an overview of what they're looking at. It's like introducing your central message before you deliver the rest of your talk, and it will make the details far more meaningful.

   Frequently the central message of your visual aid is contained in the title.

3. **Talk to a listener.** As you describe the visual, always talk to your listeners. If you need to refresh your memory about what is on the visual aid, pause, look at the visual, then look back at a listener and continue talking.

This is the hardest thing to remember when you work with visual aids. Most of us have a tendency to look at the visual when we discuss it, but that breaks our contact with the listeners.

TIP

Try to stand to the right of a visual aid (to the left, from the audience's point of view). The reason is that listeners read from left to right. That way, their eyes start with you, and you remain the center of attention as they read the visual.

4. **Avoid the Statue of Liberty position.** As you introduce the visual, it's a good idea to point to it, but most visuals should be simple enough so that you don't need to continue to point to them as you discuss them.

Too many speakers get locked in a Statue of Liberty position, which is extremely tiring and often prevents them from using gestures. If you have a bullet slide, simply refer to each point as "bullet one," or "bullet two."

If you're using a graph or chart, you can tell the audience where the information is located by saying: "in the upper corner," or "on the top." Or you can point to it periodically instead of keeping your arm locked in the Statue of Liberty position.

CAUTION: POINTERS AND LASER LIGHTS

Speakers regularly use pointers and laser lights to focus the attention of their listeners on specific aspects of a visual aid. Unfortunately, these devices are often far more trouble than they're worth.

Many speakers begin twirling their pointers like batons, when they aren't using them, which can be distracting to their listeners. It also prevents the speaker from using gestures effectively to add energy to a presentation.

While laser lights can be useful, they're a dead giveaway for any speaker suffering from nervousness: The laser beam will shake when the speaker points it toward the visual aid. The attention of the audience is now drawn away from the visual to the speaker's case of nerves.

CONSIDER HANDING OUT HARD COPIES

Presenters often ask whether they should distribute hard copies of their visuals at the start of a presentation. In some cases, the audience may be expecting hard copies, so you have little choice but to meet their expectations.

Where you do have a choice, however, don't hand out copies of your visual aids before you begin speaking. There are good reasons for avoiding this practice:

- Listeners will invariably start reading your handouts instead of paying attention to you. This undermines your effectiveness as a speaker.

- Listeners often look ahead and begin reading the hard copy of a visual aid before you reach it in your presentation. They may interrupt and ask questions about the visual before you're ready to deal with it.

- If you wanted to leave a visual out of your presentation it would be almost impossible if the audience already had copies of your visual aids.

If you want to distribute handouts, wait until the presentation is over. You don't necessarily have to provide a full set of hard copy visuals; many speakers include only the most important ones. It's a good way to make sure your listeners remember the main points of your talk.

Don't Use Visuals as Notes

Some speakers use many visual aids because they rely on them as notes. The unfortunate audience is then forced to look at far too many boring visuals.

If you need notes, use them. Write down a few key words for each idea you plan to deliver, then put the notes on the podium and refer to them as necessary. This will enable you to drastically reduce the number of slides you use in a presentation and save your listeners from visual burnout.

The 30-Second Recap

In this lesson you learned the best methods of working with visual aids in a presentation.

LESSON 12
Make It Simple

In this lesson you learn how to speak in clear, simple language so your audience will immediately comprehend your message.

Political leaders often open themselves to criticism because they talk in doublespeak so no one can understand what they're saying. While these standards may be all that we expect from politicians, we should expect far more from ourselves whenever we give a business presentation.

Our goal should always be to present even the most difficult ideas as clearly as possible. A formal presentation doesn't mean that you should resort to ponderous, $50 words that go over the heads of your listeners.

Newspaper reporters are taught to write at a sixth-grade reading level, not because their entire audience is at that level, but so that readers can grasp the meaning of what they read quickly and easily.

The same thing goes for your presentations. When good speakers phrase a sentence or select a word to deliver to their listeners, their guide is: keep it simple and short.

SPEAK NATURALLY

One manager began his presentation this way:

> A vulnerability comparison of the basic and upgraded chemical spill response system was performed to address a DOT requirement and to examine the impact of the system upgrades on the vulnerability of this facility in case of a chemical incident.

If you're wondering what the speaker was saying, so were the listeners. The message was, in fact, quite simple, but the speaker used far too many complicated words to deliver it. Compactly phrased, the message was

> We compared the new chemical response system with the old one to see if the new system was better.

Instead of using 40 words, the speaker could have said the same thing in only 19—less than half that number. Instead of using words like *upgraded, vulnerability,* and *chemical incident,* the speaker could have communicated in a simple, conversational style.

CAUTION

Don't impress—express. Don't try to impress your listeners with the extensiveness of your vocabulary. Just express yourself in everyday, conversational language.

A talk is just that—talking, so you should speak just as you would if you were talking to another person across the desk. Speeches should be like conversations, not filled with pompous-sounding, ambiguous words that leave the audience trying to guess your meaning.

USE THE ACTIVE VOICE

Most business communication seems to occur in the passive voice. The subject is being acted on by the verb.

Examples:

> The *man was hit* by the girder.
>
> The new *project was started* by the team in the second quarter.

Many speakers not only use the passive voice, they also like to depersonalize their information as much as possible.

Example:

A decision was made to reduce our marketing budget.

Perhaps the speaker doesn't want us to know who made the decision. That way, in case something goes wrong, no one will be blamed for it.

There is nothing inherently wrong with using the passive voice. If, however, you're trying to persuade your audience to take action, the passive won't do it; it's much too weak. Instead, you need to speak in the active voice.

When you use the active voice the subject is doing the acting.

Here are two examples comparing the passive and active voice.

Active: The manufacturing team should put on a third shift to handle the increased workload.

Passive: A third shift should be put on by the manufacturing team to handle the increased workload.

Active: The company should spend more money to market its new products in Europe.

Passive: More money should be spent by the company to market its new products in Europe.

In each case, the active is stronger and more forceful than the passive. It also uses fewer words. If you expect to do any convincing, especially if your listeners are skeptical, use the active voice. It will give your words far more impact.

WATCH OUT FOR JARGON

Many presentations are filled with a form of language called *jargon.* It's English, all right, but the words don't really mean very much because they've been so overused. You've heard some of these words:

synergy, bottom line, paradigm shift, proactive, touch base, think outside the box, win-win, leverage, reengineering the company

PLAIN ENGLISH

> **Jargon** is the obscure and often pretentious language of a special activity or group. There's no need to resort to meaningless business jargon when you speak. Use standard English. The English language is filled with a great variety of powerful words.

One organization became so tired of listening to these words that several employees designed a jargon bingo game. Each time a speaker at a meeting used jargon, participants marked it off on their bingo sheet. The first one to fill in five squares vertically, horizontally, or diagonally won. It was something they did to pass the time while they tried to concentrate on a boring presentation.

SHOULD YOU AVOID ACRONYMS?

Every profession and organization uses technical terms and *acronyms.* While acronyms cannot be avoided, don't assume that everyone will understand what they mean when you include them in your presentation.

PLAIN ENGLISH

> An **acronym** is a word formed by the first letters of words in a phrase. For example, *radar* is an acronym for radio detecting and ranging.

Whenever you introduce an acronym, explain what each of the letters represents. There's nothing worse than listening to a speaker who sprinkles a speech with acronyms and never tells the audience what they stand for. Some listeners will feel left out, excluded from those "people in the know" who supposedly understand what you're saying. As a result, they ignore the rest of the presentation.

MAKE IT CONVERSATIONAL, WITH PRONOUNS

Many speakers make their presentations unnecessarily formal by never using a personal pronoun. They constantly talk about "the company," "the organization," and "the department."

In the military services, speakers were accustomed to using phrases like "the command has recommended," and "the facility has decided." You'll be delighted to know that, according to recent directives in the armed forces, speakers are now expected to use more informal language in their presentations to make them more listener-friendly.

CAUTION

If your presentation has very few personal pronouns, or none at all, chances are it's much too stiff for the occasion.

Personal pronouns like *we, our, I,* and *you* are supposed to be part of every communication, whether oral or written. Perhaps it's time for people who work in the private sector to address a group as if they were talking to someone across the lunch table, and keep their language informal and conversational.

DEFLATE YOUR VOCABULARY

Why use big words, when you can say something in plain English? Evaluate your next presentation to determine whether you're planning to use any of the words in the following list. If so, replace them with ones that are simpler.

TIP

The next time you attend a presentation, listen carefully to the speaker's choice of words. Does he or she try to impress you with high sounding words and phrases or rely on down-to-earth language? Which approach works better for you and communicates the message most effectively?

Big	Simpler	Big	Simpler
accompany	go with	accomplish	do
accorded	given	accrue	add
adjacent to	next to	advantageous	helpful
allocate	give	apparent	clear
ascertain	find out	attain	meet, reach
caveat	warning	comprise	include
commence	begin	component	part
deem	believe	designate	choose
effect changes	make changes	employ	use
enumerate	count	evident	clear
expiration	end	facilitate	help
finalize	finish	function	act, role
identical	same	implement	carry out
inception	start	in order to	to
initial	first	in proximity	near
interface with	meet	in reference to	regarding
magnitude	size	methodology	method
optimum	best	promulgate	issue
pursuant to	by, per	remuneration	pay
subsequent	next, later	terminate	end
transmit	send	utilize	use

REMOVE NONWORDS FROM YOUR TALK

Some speakers punctuate their presentations with nonwords, including: *ah, um,* and *you know,* between each thought. The constant use of such nonwords can become very distracting to listeners. One of the best ways to eliminate this problem is by practicing effective eye contact. Instead of saying *um*, pause between thoughts for a second of silence. Move your eyes from one listener to another, then start speaking again. You'll reduce the number of nonwords in your talk almost immediately.

CHOOSE YOUR WORDS CAREFULLY

From time to time, I hear speakers make embarrassing mistakes by using one word when they mean to say something else. Sometimes the same mistakes show up on a visual aid. Practicing your talk in front of a friend or family member can help you catch errors like the following.

Common Errors			
affect	have an influence	**effect**	result; to bring about
allusion	reference to something	**illusion**	a mistaken perception
anecdote	story, personal experience	**antidote**	medicine to fight disease
appraise	measure, assess the value	**apprise**	inform in detail, notify
desert	dry, sandy area	**dessert**	final course of a meal
formally	in a dignified manner, according to the rules	**formerly**	previously, in the past
ingenious	clever, very skillful	**ingenuous**	innocent, naïve
moral	good; the lesson of a story	**morale**	spirit, sense of well-being
personal	individual, personal	**personnel**	the employees in a department
uninterested	not interested, don't care	**disinterested**	neutral

THE 30-SECOND RECAP

In this lesson you learned how to select the best words to deliver the information in your presentation.

LESSON 13

Banish Those Butterflies

In this lesson you learn how to deal with stage fright when you give a speech.

The CEO of a large communications firm once explained how she dealt with pressure situations, like standing up and giving formal presentations.

As a child, she recalled, she played competitive tennis and somebody would always tell her, "You have such composure." At least that's how she looked on the outside. "Inside, I was dying, either because it's the beginning of a match and I'm so nervous I want to get sick, or I'm thinking, 'I'm about to lose this match in the third set.'"

Through competitive sports, she added, "I learned how to manage the balance between the adrenaline, which is helpful, and the wanting to be sick." It's that burst of adrenaline that she still relies on to pump her up whenever she has to address a large group of people.

THINK OF BUTTERFLIES AS ADRENALINE

Most of us feel butterflies when we stand before an audience. The founder of a large nonprofit organization, who had addressed hundreds of groups, admitted that she always felt very nervous before the start of her speech.

The butterflies, or *stress,* we feel also produces the adrenaline rush that can help us become successful. It gives us a quick burst of energy that we can channel into delivering our presentations. The trick is to let the adrenaline do its job and not let the sick feeling in the pit of our stomach overcome us when we look out at the room full of listeners who seem to be hanging on every word.

PLAIN ENGLISH

> **Stress** is a heightened mental state produced in response to a threat, either real or imagined, like thinking that the audience may start laughing when you start to speak.

Don't worry about your dry mouth and moist palms. Remember that hundreds of people have been exactly where you are. They overcame it and so can you. There's a five-step process that will help you beat the butterflies and deliver a successful presentation.

STEP ONE: PREPARE, PREPARE, PREPARE

When it comes to preparing for a presentation, many people much prefer to procrastinate. Then, at almost the last minute, they start to panic. That panic carries over into the actual delivery itself and reduces its effectiveness.

Earlier lessons have outlined all the stages in planning a presentation. These include defining your central message and the meaning of the message, which you may accomplish quickly. Others, like gathering evidence, organizing the material, and developing your visual aids, are far more time-consuming. To stay focused, develop a schedule for your presentation.

First, figure out how many hours or days you need for each step. Many speakers discover that they should have started their preparation much sooner, and they may already be short on time. And remember to be generous in case some unforeseen emergencies arise. For example, you may need to take a business trip that will cut into your preparation time.

ork backward from the day of the presentation to the date where you should begin working on it. Put each step on the schedule in the order in which it should be done.

> **CAUTION**
>
> Use a schedule and stay on it. Try to schedule a short block of time every day to prepare your presentation. Make it a high priority. Preparation usually takes far longer than you think it will.

You may work on some steps, like preparing your visual aids, while you're developing the opening, body, and closing of your talk.

The planning stage is the most important part of any preparation. By rushing through it, you can easily make embarrassing mistakes that will lessen the impact of your presentation.

Remember this rule: Don't procrastinate: Plan and prepare! It's the best way to reduce your nervousness on the day of the presentation.

STEP TWO: PRACTICE YOUR DELIVERY

Make sure you leave enough time in your schedule to practice your presentation before delivering it. If something doesn't sound quite right when you give your presentation, it's too late to do anything about it. Chances are that your stage fright will get worse, and everyone will know it by your quavering, shaky voice.

A much more effective approach is to build in one or two practice sessions for yourself a day or two before the presentation. Stand in front of a mirror and rehearse your delivery, using the verbal, visual, and vocal skills.

If you feel awkward delivering your central message, change the wording. If your gestures look weak, raise your energy level.

To evaluate your strengths and weaknesses you may want to videotape yourself and review the tape, making any necessary adjustments in your delivery.

Another option is to practice in front of colleagues or family members who can give you immediate feedback. Several practice sessions may be necessary until you've eliminated any serious problems and brought your delivery to a high level of excellence.

 TIP

> If you don't have a video camera, try taping yourself on an audiotape recorder. You'll be able to evaluate your vocal energy and verbal skills and make any necessary improvements in advance.

There's an adage that practice makes perfect. That may be an over-statement, but practice will certainly make improvements in your presentation. It'll help you feel more comfortable with your delivery and reduce your stage fright on presentation day.

STEP THREE: MEET THE AUDIENCE

If I'm feeling nervous before speaking to an unfamiliar audience, I often try to chat with a few people as they enter the room. I introduce myself and try to find out something about them. By getting to know some of my listeners, I'll see some familiar faces in the audience when I stand up to speak. When I deliver my opening I try to concentrate on these listeners, who seem almost like friends.

The opening, of course, is the most important part of the presentation. This is when you can least afford to sound nervous. Yet the beginning of a talk is also when you're most likely to feel unsettled.

Arrive early to a presentation and meet a few of your listeners informally before the talk begins. You'll feel more at ease as you start to speak.

STEP FOUR: UNLEASH YOUR ENERGY

The stress that comes from looking out at a large audience awaiting the start of your presentation unlocks adrenal energy in your system. It can take the form of sweaty palms and rubbery legs, or you can use that adrenaline far more productively. Simply channel it into your gestures and use it to increase your visual energy.

Channeling adrenal energy accomplishes two things: It dissipates much of your nervousness, and it enables you to open the presentation with a high level of energy. That will capture the attention of your audience.

CAUTION

Don't let nervousness paralyze you. The vocal and visual energy you need in your opening will not be high enough. Unfortunately, this can create a poor impression with the audience and undermine the effectiveness of the entire presentation.

If you're feeling nervous at the start of a talk, the last thing you may want to do is increase your energy level. It will probably take you out of your comfort zone. But raising your energy works.

Use your gestures to emphasize key points and to describe important concepts in your talk. You'll be carried along on a high wave of enthusiasm that will immediately make you feel better while adding extra power to your presentation.

STEP FIVE: USE EYE CONTACT

If you want to increase your level of nervousness, try scanning the audience at the beginning of your talk. Your eyes will be taking in so much visual stimulation that your brain will rapidly feel overwhelmed.

All those people, all those eyes will be staring back at you. It's enough to activate our primitive fight-or-flight response. Since we can't fight, our first inclination is to run out of the room as fast as possible. Of course, you can't do that either. So you just become more and more nervous.

Remember the principles of eye contact discussed in Lesson 5, "Eye-Contact Communication." Pick a single set of eyes, perhaps someone you know or a person you met before the beginning of the presentation. Then start speaking. That turns your presentation into a one-to-one conversation. You're just talking to another person. It's the same as having a dialogue across the desk.

Keep repeating the same procedure throughout your talk. As if by magic, the rest of the audience seems to disappear, at least momentarily, and you're concentrating on just one person at a time.

Many speakers admit that this is the technique they find most helpful in decreasing their level of nervousness. They also remind themselves that the people in the audience are usually on their side. Listeners don't enjoy seeing anyone fail. Especially if many of them are speakers themselves, they usually have empathy for you and want you to succeed just as much as you do. Keep this in mind, and it will help boost your confidence when you make a presentation.

THE 30-SECOND RECAP

In this lesson you learned a five-step process for dealing with stage fright.

LESSON 14

Dealing with the Details

In this lesson you learn the importance of handling the logistics of your presentation: being on time, checking the audiovisual equipment, and arranging the room.

All of us have probably experienced that momentary panic when we realize that we may not have left ourselves enough time to travel to an important appointment. Then we get caught in traffic, and we know that we'll be late. This is especially embarrassing if you're scheduled to speak at a large conference.

There's nothing more nerve-racking than rushing into a room full of people who have been waiting impatiently for you to arrive. Your entire talk gets off on the wrong foot. Instead of beginning with a powerful opening, you're forced to apologize to your listeners for being late.

One of the most important responsibilities of any speaker is knowing the schedule and keeping to it.

TIME FLIES

No matter how carefully you've prepared and rehearsed your presentation, it won't be as effective if you arrive late to deliver it. Arriving on time should be a top priority. The following suggestions may sound fairly obvious, but you'd be surprised how many speakers overlook them.

- Make sure you know the date of your speech. You wouldn't be the first speaker to get confused and miss the date of your talk or arrive a day early. Remember to call a week or so in advance just to confirm the date. Sometimes dates are changed and the conference planners forget to inform everyone.

- Leave yourself plenty of time to arrive at a speaking engagement. Call ahead to find out how long it should take you to get there. Then add at least a third more time in case of unexpected delays.

- Be sure you know where you're supposed to speak. So many hotels and conference centers sound the same that it's easy to mix up one place with another and arrive at the wrong location.

- Get a good set of directions to your destination. Call the event planner or consult one of the services on the Internet that can map out a route for you.

TIP

Try to arrive at your speaking engagement early enough to give yourself time to check out the room as well as any equipment you may be using during your presentation.

CHECK OUT THE ROOM

When listeners are comfortable, they're far more likely to pay attention to your presentation. Their comfort is often determined by the conditions in the room where you're speaking. Before the day of your presentation, call ahead and ask some questions about the room, such as ...

- **How large is it?** The room should be big enough to easily accommodate the number of participants that are expected to attend your talk. If the room is too small, they'll be uncomfortable.

- **Where are the restrooms located?**

- **Can I control the temperature?** There's nothing worse than a room that's too hot or too cold, especially when there's nothing you can do about it. Ideally your room should have its own temperature controls that you can operate yourself. If not, you should know how to contact a service technician who can adjust the temperature in the room for you.

- **Will there be refreshments?** If you're scheduled to give a lengthy presentation or a half-day workshop, you may want to take periodic breaks. When light refreshments are available near the workshop room, the breaks become far more enjoyable. Refreshments not only reinvigorate your audience, they can give you a renewed burst of energy to continue your presentation.

- **What is the seating arrangement?** There are several ways to arrange the seating in a room. Some speakers want a classroom arrangement, with all the chairs in long rows. For a smaller group, you may prefer a few tables arranged in a more intimate U-shape. However, if you're planning team activities, separate tables with chairs grouped around them may be the best arrangement for your presentation. Have the room set up to your specifications in advance.

CAUTION

> Keep your cool. Sometimes there's little you can do to change a room that doesn't meet your expectations. Explain the problem to your listeners and ask them to work with you to make the best of a difficult situation.

There's no guarantee, of course, that the room conditions will always conform to your requests. But by arriving at your presentation substantially ahead of schedule, there may be time for you to make some adjustments; for example, changing the seating arrangement or finding a larger or smaller room if necessary. It will make the presentation far more pleasant for your listeners while giving you a far greater chance of success.

DOUBLE-CHECK THE EQUIPMENT

Many presentations have broken down because of some kind of equipment failure. While you can't eliminate every problem, anticipating them can save you a great deal of trouble later while you're giving your talk. When it comes to equipment, Murphy's Law is always operating. Here are a few steps to help you deal with it:

If you're planning to use an overhead projector, take an extra lightbulb with you. Overhead lightbulbs have a way of blowing out just when you need them the most. Some projectors have a backup bulb.

Arrive at your speaking engagement early to check out the projector. Find out whether it has two bulbs and if both of them are working. If one bulb is already bad, replace it with the spare you brought.

If you've decided to present a series of slides with a laptop computer, as a safety measure, create a backup slide presentation on an extra disk. Sometimes slide programs develop a glitch on the day you're supposed to show them. Test out the disk in advance to make sure it's running smoothly.

Try out the projection equipment for the slides before beginning your presentation. If there's any problem, find an audiovisual technician and obtain new equipment.

 TIP

> If you use overheads, number the transparencies. In case you drop them and they get out of order, it will help you put them back in sequence.

If you're using a microphone, try it out in advance to make sure it's operating properly. It may be attached to a podium, or it may be a small, portable device that you can pin onto your clothing. Some microphones produce loud feedback, which interferes with your presentation; it can be very annoying when you're trying to speak. Adjust the microphone or, if you can't, ask an audiovisual technician to provide a replacement.

REMEMBER THE LITTLE THINGS

Don't overlook the details that go into planning a presentation. It's easy to become so involved in developing your message or preparing your visual aids that you forget about a little thing that's necessary to deliver them effectively.

Remember to check those mundane details, such as when and where you're supposed to speak, the setup and size of the room, and the reliability of the equipment you'll be using. All these factors are essential to making your presentation a success.

THE 30-SECOND RECAP

In this lesson you learned about some important logistical considerations to remember whenever you give a presentation.

LESSON 15
Ten-Point Presentation Primer

In this lesson you learn how to deliver a presentation that will get you an ovation from your listeners.

Successful oral communication depends on a three-step process:

- **Preparation** Includes defining your central message and its meaning to the listeners, gathering and organizing your evidence, designing dialogue questions, and creating visual aids.

- **Practice** Involves rehearsing your presentation in front of a mirror, video camera, tape recorder, or small audience of family or coworkers.

- **Presenting** Is the actual delivery of your talk—applying all the efforts you made in the presentation's development stages when you stand up to address your listeners.

Perhaps the best way to describe the last step, presenting, is to compare it to playing a round of golf after you've finished hitting balls on the driving range. When you finally get up on the first tee, you're not entirely sure you'll be able to duplicate those long, straight drives you may have been hitting in practice. Relax. Even the pros feel nervous in tournament play. When they do, professionals concentrate on all the fundamentals they've learned on the golf course. Do what they do: Recall all the key points in this book, learn and practice the 10 points described in this lesson, and soon, hearing applause will be par for the course.

Route to Success

getting ready to speak, focus on the task at hand and remind yourself that you've done everything possible to make the presentation a success. You'll probably still experience some nervousness, which is only natural. Remember to use that adrenal energy to your advantage by injecting more power into your presentation.

TIP

> Most listeners come to a presentation ready to give you their attention, at least for a few minutes. But that may be all you have, so make the most of it. Start your talk at a high energy level.

As you begin to speak, these 10 pointers will help ensure that not only your message, but you, the speaker, will make a lasting impression on your audience.

Point One: Make Eye Contact

As you approach the podium, it's easy to feel momentarily overwhelmed when you look out at all the people in your audience. Direct your attention to one person and a single set of eyes and turn your presentation into a one-to-one conversation.

Speak to a single person, even while you're saying words that are meant for the entire audience. Don't forget that while you're looking at one person, others seated nearby believe you're looking at them, too. Once you've completed the first sentence, find another set of eyes and continue speaking.

It's easy to forget this technique and try to look at everyone. Don't; your talk won't be as powerful.

POINT TWO: OPEN THE CHANNELS

Many speakers focus on the words. They want to make sure that everything they say comes out just right. Studies reveal that what listeners remember most is not the words, but your delivery. Audiences are far more forgiving than you think. They will tolerate stumbles, pauses, and hesitations. So start your presentation by opening up all the channels—the verbal, the visual, and the vocal.

Beginning with your hands locked together and your voice at the level of a dull monotone is no way to command the attention of your audience. Let them know at the outset that they're in the presence of a powerful speaker, one who commands authority. You undoubtedly know more about your subject than they do. Speak with all the energy you can muster!

POINT THREE: CREATE A RHYTHM

Unless your talk is extremely short, it's impossible to maintain a high level of energy throughout it. You'll be exhausted and your audience will be worn out, too.

Good talks are like the tides that ebb and flow. Your energy should be high at the opening. This is the time to make a good first impression. High energy also helps dissipate your *performance anxiety.*

PLAIN ENGLISH

Performance anxiety is that natural uneasiness we feel before performing any difficult task in front of other people.

Throughout your talk, however, the energy level can go up and down. This enables you to emphasize certain key ideas that the audience should remember.

Close your talk at a high level of energy, especially as you repeat your central message and deliver a call to action.

POINT FOUR: ENERGIZE WITH GESTURES

If you look at your listeners and they seem to be losing interest, your energy level has probably begun to sag. Increasing your gestures can pick up the entire presentation.

It's very difficult to speak in a monotone while you're gesturing emphatically. A high level of visual energy will increase your vocal energy. Suddenly your presentation seems reinvigorated, the audience is brought back to life, and you are their center of interest again.

Unfortunately, you can't wait too long to apply this technique. A talk that proceeds at the same slow, quiet pace far into its body may be beyond rescue. By the time you reach the conclusion, all the energy in the world may not succeed in resuscitating your listeners.

Don't expect that the verbal channel will carry you through a presentation. Your listeners need stimulation for their eyes and ears as well. Give them what they need.

POINT FIVE: USE DIALOGUE QUESTIONS

Dialogue questions can serve a variety of purposes if you let them. They get the listeners involved in your presentation. By hearing what your audience says, you can also gauge their temperature: how they stand on the issue and what they think of your ideas. Perhaps it confirms your opinion that they're eager for a change, or you may pick up some hesitation in a few of your listeners. That may indicate that you need to work even harder to "sell" your message.

CAUTION

Don't be a control freak. You don't have to know exactly what the audience may say, and it's usually quite easy to summarize their responses with a general statement and segue back to your talk.

After you listen to their responses, summarize them briefly. You might use phrases such as: "I can see you have a wide range of opinions on this subject," or, "It helps me to know how you feel about this issue." Then go back to your talk.

POINT SIX: DON'T PANIC

Sometimes your talk may be flowing along smoothly and suddenly you can't remember your next idea. It's easy to push the panic button, but it's the worst thing you can do to your presentation. Instead, take a second or two and refer to your notes. Or if the next idea is sitting on a visual aid, turn and look at it. It gives you a little breathing room.

Don't be afraid of silences or feel you must apologize to your audience for them. They weren't expecting perfection, anyway. A brief pause will appear only natural to them, although it may seem like an eternity to you.

POINT SEVEN: GO WITH THE FLOW

Suppose you're the third or fourth speaker on a program and the conference planner asks if you can shorten your talk substantially because the other presenters ran too long. That's not a difficult problem if you've organized your talk around a central message. Open with your message. It is the key idea that you want to deliver, and everything else is just supporting information.

Then cut down the amount of evidence you plan to deliver and make sure that your most important supporting data come first in the presentation. You can easily fit your talk into the new time slot.

POINT EIGHT: KNOW THE EQUIPMENT

There's nothing more upsetting than presenting your audiovisual aids and fumbling with the hardware as you try to operate it. Overhead projectors never seem to have the on-off button in the same location, and brands of projection systems for PowerPoint slides run differently.

The message is simple: Familiarize yourself with the audiovisual equipment before you start to use it. If you look like a klutz up there with the technical hardware, your credibility and professionalism may be damaged in the eyes of your audience.

POINT NINE: NEVER MEMORIZE PRESENTATIONS

Trying to memorize a speech will almost surely land you in trouble. You're likely to forget a line, which will throw off the rest of your talk, and you may draw a blank on what you're supposed to say.

Concentrate on the thoughts you want to deliver, not the words. The likelihood is that if you present a speech more than once, some phrases will remain in the talk; others will disappear, to be replaced by better ones.

The audience will remember very few of your words; they'll remember your ideas. Write them out as notes and refer to them as necessary.

TIP

> Some speakers rely on memory aids such as acronyms created out of a series of words that summarize or begin their main ideas. This approach may help you the next time you deliver a talk.

POINT TEN: EVALUATE YOURSELF

After you finish a talk, take stock of your delivery. Evaluate your mastery of the three channels of communication.

Don't criticize yourself. Begin by focusing on what you did right. Then look at areas where you may need improvement. Set goals for yourself. Perhaps you should try to double your vocal energy next time you speak.

Solicit feedback from listeners who attended your presentation. Don't simply ask them whether they liked the talk. Most people will say yes because they don't want to offend you. But this tells you nothing.

Instead, ask them to comment specifically on your use of eye contact, the clarity of your central message, your energy level, your visual aids, and so on. A little probing will often result in some useful feedback that will help you the next time you give a talk.

The goal, of course, is to realize your full potential and become the best speaker you can be, to even receive a standing ovation when you finish your presentation.

The 30-Second Recap

In this lesson you learned about 10 points that can improve your delivery of a presentation.

LESSON 16

Handling Questions and Answers

In this lesson you learn how to handle a question-and-answer session in a way that will impress your audience.

The tall, gray-haired CEO had just completed a nearly flawless presentation about the company's reorganization plan. Then he opened the floor to questions.

A listener in the front row put up his hand. "You've told us everything except what we want to know most of all," he said. "How many of us are going to lose our jobs in the reorganization?"

The CEO attempted a smile but he was clearly uncomfortable. He tried to deal with the question, but his response sounded vague.

The listener shot back. "You're not leveling with us. What are you trying to hide?"

The CEO's face became flushed. He denied the listener's accusation and spoke in glowing terms about the upcoming changes and how they would improve the company. "I hope I've answered your question," he said.

"No, you haven't," the listener said angrily, rising from his seat. "All of us are still waiting to hear about the numbers. How many jobs are you going to eliminate?"

"Frankly, there's been no decision, yet," the CEO said. But the employee in the front row wasn't satisfied. He started to ask another question.

"I'm sorry," the CEO said, backing away from the podium. "I have to go." And with that, he hurriedly left the room. His entire presentation had become a shambles.

ANTICIPATE THOSE QUESTIONS

A question-and-answer session following a presentation can make or break your entire performance. If you're not ready for the questions, you can look like a fool; or worse, a dissembler. And you can lose control of your entire talk to someone in the audience who is trying to get the better of you.

As you prepare for a presentation, don't forget to rehearse for questions and answers. That means trying to anticipate the questions and develop credible answers to them. You can usually guess what some of the questions are likely to be, so there's no excuse for not being ready to answer them.

You can do something as simple as jotting down a list of possible questions and composing your answers. You can also rehearse the session with family members or coworkers.

TIP

Imagine that you're the president of the United States about to hold a news conference. With the help of your advisors, you prepare by anticipating the questions you're likely to be asked, and rehearsing your answers.

Remember, the very last impression that the audience will have of your presentation is likely to be the question-and-answer session that comes at the end of your talk. It should be just as strong as the rest of your performance.

LEARN THE FIVE-STEP APPROACH

Rehearsing for a question-and-answer session will make you feel more comfortable when you stand in front of an audience. When it actually comes time to deal with their questions, here's a five-step approach that can be very helpful.

STEP ONE: THE OPENING

Begin the session by telling your audience that you have a specific amount of time to handle questions—5 minutes, 15 minutes, whatever it is. Then ask the listeners if they have any questions.

As you do so, raise your hand. That indicates to the audience that you'd also like them to raise their hands when they ask questions instead of just shouting them out. This technique gives you greater control over the session.

STEP TWO: LISTENING

The question-and-answer session is one of the few times in a presentation when you're expected to listen instead of speak. As the first listener asks a question, listen all the way through.

As speakers, our tendency is to begin composing an answer before the listener has finished asking the question. Perhaps it comes from our days in elementary school, when some of us raised our hands to answer a question before the teacher had finished asking it. If the question wasn't what we thought it would be and the teacher called on us, it was very embarrassing if we didn't know the answer.

Don't start thinking about your answer until the listener has finished asking the question. It may not be the question you're anticipating, or you may not understand it, especially if the listener is not entirely fluent in English.

If you're not sure of the question, say so. Then, ask the listener to repeat it.

STEP THREE: REPHRASING THE QUESTION

Before you answer a question, rephrase it. This enables anyone in the room who may not have heard the question to know what it is. There is nothing worse for your audience than listening to your answer without having heard the question. The answer rarely makes very much sense.

In addition, rephrasing the question gives you several additional seconds to frame your answer. This may help you sound more knowledgeable.

Rephrasing does not mean repeating. For instance, if you presented a new program, someone may ask: "You haven't outlined the costs of what you propose. Are they likely to be high or low?" It takes too long to repeat the entire question. Instead, you can simply say: "You asked about costs," or, "regarding the costs of my program," or just "costs." This sums up the question in a few key words for your listeners.

Suppose a listener has asked you a provocative question. Then you should try *neutralizing* it.

PLAIN ENGLISH

Neutralizing a question does not mean changing it. Your listeners will immediately recognize what you are trying to do and you'll lose credibility. Instead, remove the pejorative terms—neutralize them—and answer the question in the way that suits your purpose.

We all know the old story about a senator who was asked by a reporter: "Senator, when did you stop beating your wife?" Trying to answer that question would make it seem like there was some truth in it. Instead, the senator rephrased and neutralized the question: "You asked about the relationship I have with my wife."

Step Four: Answering the Question

Begin your answer by making eye contact with the listener who asked the question. Then involve other members of the audience by making eye contact with them. As you come to the end, don't look back at the person who asked you the question. Finish your answer by making eye contact with someone else. This may be a difficult technique to remember but it can be extremely useful. Why?

If a listener has asked you a provocative question, and you complete your answer by making eye contact with the questioner, it's an open invitation for him or her to try to embarrass you again. The best tactic is to ignore the questioner, and it's much easier to do if you're looking at someone else when you finish your answer. Otherwise, the entire session can become a repartee between you and the questioner, who may eventually get the upper hand. Remember the employee at the beginning of this lesson who drove the CEO from the podium.

CAUTION

If the key decision-maker wants to keep asking you questions, you may have no choice but to keep going back and answering them. This person must be fully satisfied or your presentation may not be successful.

Step Five: Completing the Session

Once you've come to the end of the session and answered the final question, you might say: "That's all I have time for today." At this point, you should do one more thing: Repeat your central message as well as your call to action, if you have one. Listeners remember only a small part of a presentation. You want to make sure they don't forget your most important idea.

Instead of closing with the last answer to the last question, close with your central message and call to action.

NEVER PRETEND

Adequate preparation and an effective approach to fielding questions can make you a star at every question-and-answer session, but there still may be some questions you can't handle. If you don't know the answer to a question, say so.

Never try to pretend that you have the information. Someone in the audience is likely to realize that what you're saying is incorrect. If this happens to be a key decision-maker, the credibility of your entire presentation will immediately be undermined.

Simply tell the listener that you don't know the answer but you'll find out and get back to him or her with that information within a specific time period.

TIP

Be as responsive as possible. If you need to do further research to answer a question, don't procrastinate. Get the data as soon as you can and communicate with your listener even earlier than you promised. This shows that you're trying to be responsive.

NEUTRALIZE HOSTILE QUESTIONERS

Sometimes a member of the audience may try to provoke you with a question that has nothing to do with your central message. It's simply designed to make you look uncomfortable and enable the listener to score some points or pursue his or her own agenda.

The other listeners usually know what's going on and they expect you to deal with the situation. Without being unpleasant, you can simply tell the listener that you'd be happy to take up this issue at another time after the presentation is over. But this session is not the time or the place to do it. As you finish your statement make sure you're not making eye contact with the questioner, who will try to keep talking.

In some especially heated question-and-answer sessions, a listener may stand up while asking a question and begin to approach the speaker. That is a clear attempt to take over the presentation. If this happens to you, immediately put up your hand. Then ask the listener to return to his or her seat. When someone realizes that you're not going to give up control, it's usually enough to persuade the person to sit down. The audience will usually be on your side.

Suppose a listener asks you an embarrassing question and, before you can answer it, tries to gather support for his or her position from other members of the audience. Perhaps the person says: "I know everyone here agrees with me," or specifically names several other people and says: "Tell everybody here what you think." That is another blatant attempt by a listener to take over your presentation. Before the person can go any further, make it clear that you'll only deal with his or her problem, and that if anyone else has concerns, you'll be happy to address them one by one.

STAY IN CONTROL

This is your question-and-answer session, and you should stay in charge of it at all times, whenever it occurs during your presentations. Some managers report that their listeners will not wait until the end for questions, but ask them throughout a presentation. In such cases, you must be ready to answer everyone, but after you finish each answer, always segue back into your presentation. Repeat your central message and remind your listeners of the previous points you covered before going on to introduce any new information.

The key is to always land on your feet as you answer each question and to demonstrate to the audience that this is your presentation and you know what you're talking about.

THE 30-SECOND RECAP

In this lesson you learned a proven approach to handling question-and-answer sessions successfully.

LESSON 17

One-to-One Presentations

In this lesson you learn how to deliver one-to-one presentations.

Most of us don't have the opportunity to deliver a stand-up presentation every day, or for that matter, even once a week. However, we do have plenty of occasions to speak one-to-one with coworkers: at the water fountain, in the cafeteria, or across the desk. Each is a situation for practicing the skills of effective communication.

Suppose you come up with an idea for streamlining the operations in your unit. First you might decide to walk down the hallway and try it out on one of your colleagues. If your presentation is convincing and your colleague gives you a thumbs-up, you might then present the same proposal to your supervisor.

When you talk to your supervisor, a clear, concise delivery is critically important. It's not only the best way to win approval for your proposal, it can enhance your image in the supervisor's eyes.

Perhaps you regularly make sales presentations to describe new products or services. If you want to be successful, your message must be short and easy to understand, with plenty of benefits for the potential customer.

Apply what you've learned from this book about group presentations, and follow this lesson's advice on how to make an effective one-to-one presentation.

Put Your Best Foot Forward

One-to-one presentations may be less formal than stand-up speeches. They can also be less stressful because you're usually sitting down, and you're not speaking to a big audience. Nevertheless, the criteria of good oral communication are no different.

TIP

Remember to prepare. One-to-one presentations require preparation just like formal speeches do. Work on the verbal, visual, and vocal components of your communication so they'll be as sharp as possible when you deliver your information to a listener.

In every case, you must put your best foot forward and effectively apply the same skills that you'd demonstrate in front of a large group.

Present First Things First

Whether you're presenting to your supervisor, a coworker, or a customer, one thing is almost certain. They're busy people without much extra time to listen, so you need to get to the point, and get there quickly. That means that the first step in preparing any one-to-one communication is to define your central message. Instead of sounding vague and uncertain when you speak, you'll know exactly why you're speaking and what you want to accomplish. Your listener will, too.

If you want your supervisor to fund your proposal, or a customer to buy your product, make sure they know what's in it for them (WIIFM). Sometimes, it even helps to lead off with this information and follow up with the central message. You're almost always guaranteed to get the listener's full attention.

KNOW WHAT APPEALS TO YOUR LISTENERS

Your listener analysis is relatively easy in a one-to-one presentation. But if you get it wrong and don't know what kind of evidence is most likely to convince your listener of your position, you're probably not going to accomplish your goal.

If the listener is a numbers person, include statistics. If he or she is likely to be impressed because a major competitor is doing the same thing, be sure to mention it. Always present your most important evidence early, in case you run out of time at the end.

Some listeners need a picture to persuade them. One of the most effective visual aids is a PowerPoint slide on your laptop computer. Keep the visual simple. Then, as you present it, follow the same approach that you would use in a formal presentation. Apply what you learned from earlier lessons:

- Give the listener an overview of the visual aid.

- Describe each of the details.

- Don't talk to the visual, talk to the listener.

Remember to only use visuals that can make your point better than you can do it orally.

CAUTION

> Don't push the laptop computer to the listener's side of the desk; it may be interpreted as an invasion of his or her space. Keep the computer on your side of the desk and under your control. The same rule applies if you're using a transparency.

MAKE YOUR POINTS WITH ENERGY

Energy is essential in a one-to-one presentation. Otherwise the listener won't believe that you're committed to what you're saying.

Most of us naturally use gestures when we speak to another person, but we usually use our visual energy less than we do when we speak to a large group. Keeping our hands in front of us is appropriate for a one-to-one situation.

CAUTION

Many speakers seem to forget about energy when they make one-to-one presentations. Perhaps they're afraid of coming on too strong and overwhelming the listener. Nevertheless, a high level of energy— but one appropriate to the situation—is important if you want to make your case.

Vocal energy is also important to add emphasis and meaning to your words when you're presenting one-to-one. Once again, the volume is much lower than it would be in front of a big audience. Nevertheless, the listener should never be in any doubt that you feel strongly about your message.

PRACTICE EYE CONTACT

Eye contact is a valuable visual skill when you're making a presentation across a listener's desk. If you're looking around the room as you talk, the person is likely to think that you're not interested in him or her, or, worse yet, that you're trying to hide something.

CAUTION

Eye contact may be more important in one-to-one conversations than it is when you're speaking to a large group. It's more noticeable to a single listener if you seem hesitant to look him or her in the eye. You can easily appear to be bored or indifferent and the listener will stop paying attention.

On the other hand, you can't stare at the listener throughout the entire presentation. This will only make the person feel uncomfortable; you should stop talking and break eye contact at appropriate intervals. Look down at your notes, to one side, or refer to your visual aid. Then resume your conversation.

REMEMBER TO LISTEN

One-to-one presentations don't need to be continuous monologues by the speaker. You may decide to ask an open-ended dialogue question to involve your listener or solicit information from the person. Your presentation may also leave your listener with some unanswered questions that can only be handled in a question-and-answer session.

In both of these situations, your role is to listen so that you understand the questions and can deal with them effectively. The answers may be critical to convincing your listener that your idea or your product is worth trying.

Don't fumble the presentation at the question-and-answer stage. Try to prepare yourself for possible questions. An "I don't know," or an "I'll have to find that information for you," may only leave the listener feeling that you're not really in command of your subject.

Finally, repeat your central message at the end of your presentation. If you have a call to action, make it; if you're trying to make a sale, ask for the order. Otherwise, your entire effort may have been totally useless.

MAINTAIN YOUR PERSPECTIVE

One-to-one presentations may seem more informal and relaxed than stand-up speeches, but they can be just as vital to your future. A client once explained that each talk you give is like a job interview—you're being evaluated by your audience. Keep this perspective in mind as you make a presentation across the desk. It will help you stay sharp and in charge during your delivery.

The 30-Second Recap

In this lesson you learned how to use your verbal, visual, and vocal skills to give one-to-one presentations.

LESSON 18
Listening

In this lesson you learn how to improve your listening skills.

"You aren't listening!" is a common complaint made by many people who are trying to communicate with someone else. Unfortunately, some people prefer to do all the talking and none of the listening.

In every successful communication, the speaker and the listener have had the opportunity to play both roles. While it may seem a bit unusual in a book on business presentations to include a lesson on listening, listening is an essential part of every presentation. We must listen during dialogue questions and question-and-answer sessions in order to handle them effectively.

In addition, effective listening skills enable us to read the audience and determine their reactions to our message.

CONSIDER THE VALUE OF LISTENING

As children, all of us learned the importance of *listening.* If your parents said, "Don't touch that hot stove," and you didn't pay attention you suffered the consequences. For most of us, "learning things the hard way" seemed to be a natural part of growing up. That usually meant not listening when an adult told you to do something.

PLAIN ENGLISH

Listening is paying attention to sounds; hearing with thoughtful attention.

School was a listening laboratory. Teachers stood at the blackboard and lectured. Coaches taught us the rules of a game and how to play it. Most of the information we gathered came from listening.

As an adolescent, perhaps you worked at an after-school job. Learning how to do that job usually meant getting a set of instructions, practicing what you were told, receiving feedback from a supervisor, and, you hoped, mastering the work.

Your success depended on listening. We apply the same listening skills in every job we do as adults. Studies point out that almost 50 percent of our time at work is spent listening; that nearly equals the hours we spend in reading, writing, and speaking combined.

LEARN THE LISTENING PROCESS

Human sounds bombard us from every direction. We sit in meetings, pick up voice-mail messages, watch television, and receive information over the radio. We hear these sounds, but we don't always listen to them.

Listening involves processing the sounds through our brains. First, the messages we hear must hold some interest for us. Otherwise, we simply ignore them. Much of what occurs in meetings, for example, falls into this category.

Second, we must begin to process these messages, which means visualizing what they mean, putting them into our own words, and thinking about them.

Then we begin to connect the new messages with other material: information we've heard in the past, or seen, or read about in a variety of sources such as company reports, periodicals, television, conversations with coworkers, formal presentations, and so on.

With our past knowledge and our unique experiences we put our own "spin" on the material we receive. Suppose you're attending a presentation and the speaker has just made an important statement. You might use this new idea to

- Change your perspective or reinforce your current perspective.

- Decide to do further research to find out more information.

- Respond to what you've heard by saying something to the speaker.

TIP

> Listening involves not only your ears, but your brain and your eyes as well. To respond appropriately you must hear what a person is saying, read his or her body language, and process what the person is communicating.

These are exactly the same responses we're called on to provide during a question-and-answer session. We must follow the same listening process, using precisely the same skills, to handle these sessions effectively.

OPEN ALL CHANNELS

Listening occurs on many levels. It begins with the words that someone else is using.

Suppose you've just completed a presentation on a pension and retirement health plan for your organization, and someone from the audience raises his or her hand and asks a question. It involves coverage for prescriptions. The listener could say:

Will our prescriptions be fully covered under the new plan?

or

This sounds like an attempt by management to shortchange retirees and I bet our prescriptions won't be fully covered any more, will they?

In both cases the questioner is looking for the same information, but the words are entirely different.

Something else may be different, too: the questioner's *affect.*

PLAIN ENGLISH

Affect is the feeling or emotion connected with what a person says.

The first question, for example, may be delivered in a neutral tone of voice by a questioner simply looking for clarification. Or there may be a hint of skepticism in the questioner's tone. The affect will tip you off to the person's attitude and how you choose to respond to it.

You have to be listening "between the lines" to pick up the affect. Otherwise, you may fumble your response during the question-and-answer session.

The affect of the second question, of course, is much more obvious. There will certainly be an edge to the questioner's voice, and there may be resentment or even anger in the person's tone. So you must be prepared not to ruffle the feathers of a hostile questioner.

READ THE BODY LANGUAGE

When people talk, their body language often speaks volumes—sometimes far more than their words can ever say. Take the example of a woman recounting a seemingly unimportant incident that happened many years in the past. Her mouth may begin to droop, her eyes may grow sad, and she may start twisting the ring on her finger. This body language tells you that the event is still very much alive for her and still casting a dark shadow over her life.

Watch the body language of your listeners during the dialogue questions or question-and-answer sessions in your presentation. As they're speaking, what do you see on their faces? Sometimes their facial expressions may reveal that an organizational problem is far more serious than their words are revealing, or than you could ever have imagined. Focus your attention on the speaker, and observe with your eyes as well as your ears, and you'll get all, not just part, of the message.

As pointed out in an earlier chapter, reading an audience's body language can also tell you how they're reacting to your message during a presentation:

> Is one listener smiling and nodding his or her head?

> Is another listener taking assiduous notes as you speak?

> Did a key decision-maker respond to your last visual aid with a look of knowing appreciation?

If so, then your message is having a positive impact on the audience.

BECOME A BETTER LISTENER

Although we spend a great deal of our lives listening, most of us have never taken a course in it. We learn the fundamentals of other communications skills—writing, reading, even public speaking—but not listening.

LISTEN RESPECTFULLY

Good listening begins when you put yourself in someone else's shoes. How many times have you caught yourself growing impatient while someone is relating an experience or asking a question? You want him or her to hurry up and finish. Try to imagine that you're that person. How would you like to be treated? Respond to that person the same way.

TIP

> Most people speak at 160 words per minute. But you can listen at a rate that's three times faster. During dialogue or a question-and-answer session wait for the person who's speaking to finish. Fight the tendency to stop listening, cut the person off, or let a look of impatience cross your face.

Have you ever found yourself basing your reaction to people on their surface appearances? The way they're dressed? The accents in their voices? All of us have probably been guilty of doing it from time to time. Unfortunately, the tendency to jump to conclusions can undermine the quality of our listening. It's too easy to write off people because they're different from us, and to fail to give them our full attention when they ask questions.

Give every listener the same thing you'd expect: your complete interest in what they're saying.

OVERCOME DISTRACTIONS

Effective listening can only take place in the absence of distractions; the distractions can be external or internal.

Perhaps two people in the audience are talking to each other while someone else is asking a question. One way to deal with the problem is to position yourself so that you can look at them; making eye contact with one of them may be enough to stop their conversation. If not, you might also say: "Excuse me, I can't quite hear the question." That's usually enough to handle the problem.

Some distractions can be internal. As a listener is asking a question, you may be thinking about something else. Consequently, you may not hear the question and may give a response that's incomplete, or even completely irrelevant. This will reflect badly on you. Remember, often your presentation doesn't end until you've dealt with all the questions from your audience. So banish the distractions and don't start thinking about your next meeting before you've finished with the current one.

Listening is a critical component of every successful talk.

THE 30-SECOND RECAP

In this lesson you learned about effective listening skills.

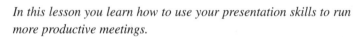

LESSON 19

Make Meetings Matter

In this lesson you learn how to use your presentation skills to run more productive meetings.

Management guru Peter Drucker points out that "One prime indicator of bad organization and time wasting is a proliferation of meetings." He might have added that the length of these meetings often allows little time for anything else, including meaningful work.

Many managers confess that so much of their day is consumed with meetings that they must stay after hours, and often far into the evenings, to catch up on important projects. Indeed, a recent survey shows that more than 50 percent of an executive's time is consumed in meetings.

According to one study, a typical corporate meeting ...

1. Is held in a conference room and lasts at least two hours.

2. Has no written agenda circulated in advance.

3. Wastes a substantial amount of time on unimportant issues.

4. Uses handouts as the most common audiovisual aids.

5. Depends for its success on the effectiveness of the leader and his or her control of the agenda.

What this study tells us is that too many meetings are unproductive and that changing this situation lies in the hands of the leader or facilitator.

DO YOU NEED A MEETING?

Perhaps the first question you need to ask as you prepare for a meeting is: Do you need to call it? Some issues can just as easily be handled via e-mail or through several telephone conversations. It saves a lot of time, and often expensive traveling, and doesn't pull people away from their desks.

 TIP

> Do your advance work. Good meetings take planning and preparation. Like effective presentations, a meeting will only accomplish its goal if you do some advance thinking before you get in there.

However, meetings do serve important functions. They enable people to

- **Bounce ideas off each other and develop new insights.** The whole is often bigger than the sum of its parts.

- **Reach consensus among key players.**   This may be essential to ensure success.

- **Listen to a report.**   This serves as a key milestone in an ongoing project.

- **Make an important decision.**   This may involve a discussion of alternatives before agreeing on a final course of action.

Just remember that, before you begin to plan a meeting, you should always consider other ways of accomplishing your goal.

DEVELOP YOUR MEETING PLAN

The problem with most meetings is that they try to accomplish too much. A successful meeting focuses around a single main idea and a single goal. They should be contained in your central message.

DEFINE THE CENTRAL MESSAGE

The central message should be clear and stated in as few words as possible. Write it out for yourself before you do anything else. Everything that occurs at the meeting should be related to that single message. For more on central messages see Lesson 2, "Define the Central Message."

DECIDE WHO SHOULD ATTEND

Meetings frequently involve far too many people. The information discussed at the meeting may not be relevant to some of them and their input is not necessary to make a decision.

 CAUTION

> Meetings can easily grow unwieldy when too many people attend them. Limit your meetings to as few attendees as possible. Think carefully about who absolutely needs to be there, and leave everyone else out.

To ensure that your central message is meaningful to the attendees, invite only those people who are essential and likely to benefit from being at the meeting.

PREPARE AN AGENDA

Once you've defined a central message, you should develop an agenda that's built around it. Agendas can be simple; just a few key points are usually enough.

Circulate your agenda in advance to give others a chance to prepare or anticipate what the meeting is likely to cover. Attendees can then begin thinking about the meeting.

The agenda is like a road map. It tells attendees where you plan to go and how you expect to get there. They must know these things to be active participants in the meeting.

If you expect people to bring some materials with them, include this information in the agenda. If one of the participants is supposed to make a presentation as part of the meeting, the agenda should indicate it.

FACILITATE EFFECTIVELY

Many of the earlier lessons about presentations also apply to meetings. Keep them in mind when you facilitate your meetings.

KEEP THE MEETING SHORT

Meetings often seem to take on a life of their own. They run far too long, wearing out most of the participants who must sit through them.

 TIP

> The best meetings have strict time limits, which usually means that they're kept short. If your central message is clear and you stick to your agenda, there's no reason why your meeting has to last a long time.

Start to build a reputation for yourself in the organization as someone who knows how to run brief meetings that don't ramble and meander all over the place. To do that you must be prepared to exercise control over a meeting when you lead it. Use the same approach you follow as a good speaker; stay in control of your presentation throughout its delivery.

Time management is critical in a meeting, but is an area where many facilitators slip up. Stay on schedule, or else you may have to skip some agenda items, or pass over some of them too hurriedly to allow for informed decisions.

OPEN WITH ALL CHANNELS

We live in a society that responds to visual images. Experts point out that the way we receive our information is 55 percent visually, 37 percent vocally, and 7 percent verbally. When you're speaking to an audience, they're not only listening to your message, they're also looking at you.

Running a meeting is similar to delivering a talk. You have to open up the three channels of communication—visual, vocal, and verbal. This means injecting energy into your presentation.

The opening is the most important part of a meeting. It's the time to deliver your central message and to make sure that every participant understands what's in it for them. It's also the place to demonstrate your commitment to achieving the goal of the meeting. That requires visual and vocal energy.

Making eye contact with participants is an effective way of making a connection with them, establishing rapport, and effectively communicating. Be sure to apply the same approach you'd use during a presentation: Deliver a thought to a set of eyes, pause, find another pair of eyes, and continue speaking.

ENCOURAGE DIALOGUE

Meetings are primarily designed to solicit participation among the people who attend them. Effective facilitators know how to encourage participants to speak but prevent discussions from going on too long or running off on a tangent that has no relationship to the meeting's central message.

The best way to elicit discussion is by asking open-ended dialogue questions:

> What is your reaction to the report?

> What can we do to improve the production operation?

> How can we find a software vendor with a successful track record?

> What information do we need to make this decision?

Again, you'll find more on handling dialogue questions in Lessons 9, "Interact with Audiences," and 16, "Handling Questions and Answers."

KEEP THE MEETING ON COURSE

A dialogue with meeting participants is essential to keeping them involved. The secret to effective dialogue is knowing how to keep it tightly focused so that the meeting doesn't run away from you.

If someone goes off on a tangent, you may need to interrupt the person. It can be done gently but effectively with a statement such as:

> I have to stop you at this point.

> I think that's very interesting, but it's not directly related to this meeting.

> I'm afraid I have to interrupt, we're running short of time.

CAUTION

> Don't wait too long to step in and cut off a participant for fear of offending him or her. If you do, the meeting may have already run away from you. Step in sooner rather than later.

Generally, the other participants will recognize what you're trying to do and support your efforts. If you don't step in, you run the risk of losing control of the meeting and sitting there helplessly while it fails to accomplish its goal.

Read Your Audience

When an attendee is talking too long, or a meeting is running out of gas, the participants will let you know it. They may not say anything; they don't have to. Just read their body language. Their lack of interest or exhaustion is written all over their faces. You can see it in their posture. They may start looking at their watches or drumming their fingers on a table.

React quickly. Get the meeting back on track and start moving it toward a successful conclusion. Otherwise, everyone is likely to walk away having accomplished nothing.

You want your meeting to accomplish the goal that you set for it.

Conclude with an Action Plan

Meetings often seem to suffer from a lack of closure. No one knows how to carry out any of the decisions reached at them, and the result is that nothing ever gets accomplished.

Your meeting should conclude with an action plan. Explain to participants what is expected of them so that you can achieve the goals you agreed on at the meeting. Set reasonable timelines to ensure that the targets are met. It's the best way to eliminate any misunderstandings and ensure that every participant is moving forward in the same direction to the same destination.

The 30-Second Recap

In this lesson you learned how to use your presentation skills to run effective meetings.

LESSON 20

Mastering the Media

*In this lesson you learn how to use your presentation skills to partici-
pate in effective interviews.*

While you're working in an organization, you may be called by a
member of the press for an interview. It might be conducted over the
telephone and used in a radio broadcast, or the information from your
interview might appear in a newspaper or magazine article.

You may be interviewed on camera, and your responses aired on local
or national news. Interviews can be conducted for a variety of purposes:

1. To provide background information for a news story

2. To supply general material on your specific organization

3. To focus on a controversial decision or project that involves
   your company

4. To provide information about you

When a reporter calls and requests an interview, your natural reaction
may be negative. It's easy to imagine yourself on a program like *60
Minutes* being grilled by a hard-nosed interviewer who's out to expose
some mistake you've made. Just remember that interviews can also
give you an opportunity to make a positive impact.

Giving an interview is a presentation just like any other. The same
public-speaking skills apply here, plus a few others, and they'll enable
you to conduct a successful interview.

PREPARE FOR THE INTERVIEW

The most important thing in any interview is to realize that this is your show, not the reporter's. Always try to stay in control, even if the reporter tries to throw you.

Once you've received the invitation to be interviewed, begin planning for it. Most interviews are short, and you'll probably have an opportunity to deliver a single central message.

After you answer each question, return to your central message so the interviewer will be sure to remember it.

TIP

Know your objectives. Start the interview with a central message and three pieces of evidence you want to get across. Then stay on track.

Anticipate the questions, just as you would if you were preparing for a question-and-answer session. You'll probably have a pretty good idea of what the reporter is likely to ask. If you need help, talk to your colleagues and rehearse your answers with them.

Be prepared with three questions that you'd like to be asked. Good interviewers will ask if there are any questions you'd like to address during the interview. When one doesn't, you can work your questions into the conversation. For example, you might answer the interviewer's question, then say, "and there's a related question that I think is equally important." Then deal with it.

ANSWER QUESTIONS WITH CARE

Once the interview begins, there are some key points to keep in mind. Whether you're on camera or being interviewed in person or over the telephone, they'll help make your interview a success.

- Most reporters are smart, outgoing people who want you to be a good interviewee. You'll get along fine as long as you're open and straightforward.

- Fill your answers with specific examples and anecdotes that illustrate your key ideas. Interviewers appreciate anecdotes because they add texture to a story.

- "No comment" is never a good answer. If you don't want to answer a question, say so, and explain why. Example: "It's up to the courts to decide, and it would be inappropriate for me to make a public statement."

- Avoid convoluted, jargon-filled language, and don't make any claims that you can't support.

- Look upon the interview as a business meeting, not a combat situation, and act as you would in any business setting.

CAUTION

> Accentuate the positive. Don't try to knock down someone else's position during an interview. Instead, concentrate on making your own case as strong as possible.

Remember that you can do much more than just avoid mistakes; you can successfully promote your central message.

BE PREPARED FOR ON-CAMERA INTERVIEWS

On the day of a television interview, wear traditional, conservative clothing. Avoid a white blouse or shirt. It's a color that shines in the camera. Select a softer color, such as blue.

You should also leave any large jewelry at home. Showy jewelry pieces can create flares in the camera lens and distract from your message.

A technician will probably pin a microphone to your clothing. Don't touch the microphone or tap your fingers on the table or desk you may be seated at. Microphones are very sensitive, and they will pick up low-level sounds.

When you're being interviewed, unless you're asked to do otherwise, look at the reporter, not at the camera.

TIP

Try not to be distracted by the camera; the camera operator knows how to position the equipment so that you'll appear natural to the audience. Whether you're on camera or off, be as relaxed as possible and don't make exaggerated gestures.

Keep your answers short, 60 seconds or less. Avoid rambling or making long digressions. The audience will find them boring.

Finally, be yourself, not some television personality you've seen on camera; you'll make a much better impression on the viewers.

BE READY FOR COMMON PROBLEMS

Interviews may not always run smoothly, especially if you're being asked to deal with a controversial issue. Here are a few common problems and how you can handle them.

PROBLEM ONE: YOU'RE ASKED A "ZINGER"

If the interviewer asks you a tough question, don't overreact. Before you answer the question, analyze it in your mind. If necessary, ask the interviewer for clarification and for the grounds on which he or she is basing the question. Try to throw it back in the interviewer's court before you begin your answer. Then rephrase the question to neutralize it, if necessary, and provide an answer.

PROBLEM TWO: YOU DON'T KNOW

If you don't know the answer to a question, there's nothing wrong in admitting that you're not the expert on the subject. Suggest someone the reporter might contact for the best information. Above all, don't try to wing it. The interviewer, who probably knows the answer, may point out your mistake and embarrass you on camera.

PROBLEM THREE: YOU MAKE A MISTAKE

If you make a mistake, don't be afraid to say so in the middle of the interview. Then go back and correct yourself. No one is expecting you to be perfect. But if you leave an incorrect impression in the mind of the interviewer or the television audience, it may hurt your message and your organization.

PROBLEM FOUR: YOU QUESTION THE QUESTION

If you think the interviewer's question is not quite right, restate it more clearly, or mention a related question that you feel is closer to the mark and answer it.

PROBLEM FIVE: THE INTERVIEWER PROVOKES YOU

If the interviewer tries to provoke you, don't demonstrate your anger. Show your willingness to discuss anything in an objective, calm way, and make sure any disagreements with the interviewer are factual, not emotional.

USE ALL YOUR SKILLS

Your words will carry you part of the way during an interview, but always remember the other channels of communication. They enable you to add emphasis and power to what you're saying.

Use hand gestures, especially when you're appearing on camera.

Research shows that people who talk with their hands on camera are perceived as being more honest and direct than those who don't. But television magnifies movements, so be sure to reduce the energy of your on-camera gestures by half of what you would use in a large conference room.

When you talk with your hands, your facial expressions become more natural. Visual energy also enables you to dissipate some of the nervousness you may be feeling as the interview begins.

MAKE IT *YOUR* INTERVIEW

Media interviews enable you to reach a broad audience. But you can only be successful if the interview accomplishes your goals.

- Know your key message before you begin the interview, and stick to it.

- Make sure the message is relevant and interesting to the audience that you're trying to reach.

- Keep your answers relatively short and always tie them back to the central message.

- Use energy to enhance the credibility of your ideas.

- Conclude the interview by reemphasizing your central message.

Practice the strategies and techniques in this lesson, and the interviews you give will be more successful every time.

THE 30-SECOND RECAP

In this lesson you learned how to use your presentation skills to handle media interviews.

LESSON 21
Continuous Improvement

In this lesson you learn how to keep your oral communication skills finely tuned.

A colleague of mine has this to say about becoming an effective public speaker: "There's some good news," he explains, "and some bad news."

The good news is that making presentations is based on a set of skills, not some innate genetic ability. Anyone can develop and refine these skills so they become better presenters.

But that's also the bad news. Once you learn these skills, you need to constantly practice them. Otherwise, like a good golf swing or accomplished piano technique, the skills atrophy and decline.

USE YOUR PRESENTATION SKILLS

It's easy to read a book and try to incorporate a set of skills into your next few presentations. You can work on the verbal channel, refining your central message, making it relevant to your listeners, and using clear, simple words to deliver your ideas.

You can open up the visual channel, using eye contact to connect with each of your listeners and obtain feedback from them during your speech. You can also raise your energy level, with gestures that describe and reinforce your message.

Finally, you can unclog the vocal channel. The human voice is a marvelous instrument that can add passion and power to your words by changing its tone and volume. Pauses and silences can also punctuate a presentation, giving it greater meaning.

Each of these skill sets can make you a better speaker, but only if you constantly remember to use them. Otherwise, your presentations won't continue to improve, they'll decline almost to the level at which they started before you read this book.

PRACTICE EVERY DAY

As you begin this section, you may be saying to yourself: "I can't give a presentation every day. So how can I expect to become a better speaker?"

TIP

It's possible to become a better speaker, but you must be willing to practice. Think of public speaking as part of your job. It's something you need to work at constantly so you can be the best.

Simple: You can practice your presentation skills every time you talk. Suppose you're having a conversation with one or two people in your office. Instead of simply focusing on your words, concentrate on your body language.

Are you practicing effective eye contact? Are you using gestures and vocal energy to reinforce your ideas? What are your facial expressions saying to your listeners? What is their body language telling you?

Raise your level of awareness as you talk to friends and family members. Each situation presents an opportunity for you to sharpen your skills.

The more conscious you are of using the three communication channels on every occasion, the more likely you'll be to open them up when you give a stand-up presentation in front of a large audience.

DON'T HIDE: SPEAK

When your supervisor asks for a volunteer to give a presentation, don't shrink into a corner; use the opportunity to improve your presentation skills.

> **CAUTION**
>
> Don't shrink from agreeing to give a presentation when asked because the idea makes you anxious. Agree to do it, and if you immediately say to yourself, "What have I done?" well, you've just given yourself a chance to become a better speaker.

There are many types of talks that you may be called on to deliver, and they're not all high-pressure situations.

THE JOB DESCRIPTION

This usually consists of describing your job, or what your functional area does, to a group of visiting customers, vendors, or others. It's a fairly low-risk presentation. All you have to do is talk about what you know best.

THE TEAM PRESENTATION

Team presentations have become very common in most organizations. Usually you'll appear onstage with other members of your team. Each person will be responsible for only one aspect of the presentation, so you'll only need to speak for a short period of time. In addition, you have the support of other team members during your delivery.

One team member is generally designated to lead off the presentation. If you feel comfortable in this role and want to deliver your talk as soon as possible, volunteer to be the first speaker.

Generally, you'll be asked to deliver the central message. Then you'll introduce the next presenter.

MEETING OR WORKSHOP FACILITATOR

Being a facilitator doesn't require you to give a long presentation. You generally set the agenda, give a short introduction, and then solicit input from other members of the meeting or workshop.

TIP

Try out low-risk situations where you can make a presentation. Gradually increase the level of difficulty until you feel comfortable standing up in front of a group.

One psychologist says she loves this type of environment because it plays to her strength. She enjoys asking open-ended dialogue questions and encouraging participants to speak. At the end, she summarizes what's been said, and if it seems appropriate, she formulates an action plan.

RUNNING A BOOTH

Many companies have booths at large conventions or trade shows. They may be run by salespeople as well as other employees who are technical experts.

Standing in a booth for an entire day gives you an opportunity to talk to a variety of people, one-to-one, or in small groups. In this situation you can use all your presentation skills.

TAKE ADVANTAGE OF VOLUNTEER ACTIVITIES

One of the best things about volunteer activities is that they give you an opportunity to try something new in a low-risk situation. Your job and your future don't depend on your performance.

Volunteering also gives you a chance to stretch yourself. You can experiment with an activity or work in a field that's far removed from your regular routine. If it turns out to be enjoyable, you can continue. If not, you can do something else.

Volunteering often provides excellent opportunities to sharpen your speaking skills. You really have very little to lose when you

- Introduce a guest speaker at a club luncheon. It's short, easy, and the spotlight is not on you, but on the speaker.

- Work as a *docent* in a museum or historic site, giving tours. You can describe paintings and artifacts, and provide historical information to groups of visitors.

PLAIN ENGLISH

A **docent** is a person being trained to become a teacher or guide.

- Read to groups of schoolchildren. You can practice your vocal and visual skills as you tell a story.

- Coach a sport and use your enthusiasm to motivate a team.

- Lead nature walks and describe the flora and fauna along the trail.

- Teach a course in your area of expertise at a local high school.

- Run a committee at a club or civic organization.

All of these activities will help you become a better speaker.

ENROLL IN PUBLIC-SPEAKING PROGRAMS

Many courses are available in public speaking. One of the best is the Focus Communications Executive Communications Program. Their Web site is www.focuscommunications.com.

Look for courses that include the following elements:

- Plenty of opportunities for you to stand up and speak. Lectures by an instructor will not help you become a better presenter.

- Feedback from the instructor and other students. You won't improve unless you know your shortcomings.

- Videotaping. If you can see yourself on camera, it will enable you to correct problems and make improvements much faster.

- A step-by-step approach. This enables you to learn about a skill, practice it, then add an additional skill. At the end of the session, you should be able to put all the skills together in a single presentation.

- Printed materials. Books, handouts, and other materials give you a ready reference source during the course and after you complete it.

Once you've finished a program, look for articles about public speaking in magazines and newspapers. You may also decide to read additional books on the topic.

Make presentation skills an area in which you're constantly learning and trying to build your expertise. You can be sure that you'll become a better speaker.

THE 30-SECOND RECAP

In this lesson you learned how to constantly improve your skills as a speaker.

APPENDIX A
Glossary

acronym A word formed from the first letters of words in a phrase, such as *radar* (radio detecting and ranging).

active voice When the subject is doing the acting.

agenda A list of things to be decided or acted on at a meeting.

central message The main point of your presentation.

close-ended question A question for which there is only one correct answer or a brief one- or two-word response.

dialogue question An open-ended question that encourages listeners to share their experiences, attitudes, or feelings on a subject.

empathy The ability to put yourself in someone else's shoes and feel what he or she does.

energy An enthusiasm and passion for your central message.

evidence Data that either proves or disproves a viewpoint, like the material presented in a court of law to prove a person's innocence or guilt.

goal of a presentation The result you want to achieve by delivering it.

ice-breaker A question that begins a dialogue or interaction between a speaker and listener(s).

meaning of the message How the central message is relevant to the listeners and what they are likely to get out of it.

mind-mapping A process of brainstorming ideas related to your central message and graphically displaying them so you can decide which ones are relevant and important.

neutralizing a question   Removing pejorative terms so you can deal with the question the way you want to.

passive voice   When the subject is being acted upon.

performance anxiety   That natural uneasiness we feel before performing any difficult task in front of other people.

scanning   A method of eye contact in which the speaker's eyes are continually moving from one person to another.

stage fright   A natural anxiety that most people feel when they get up and speak before a group of listeners.

stress   A heightened mental state produced in response to a threat, real or imagined.

template   A master slide that creates a design for each of your visual aids.

APPENDIX B

The Speaker's Notebook

Copy these forms and use them when you plan, present, and evaluate the success of your presentations.

LESSON 1

BECOME AN EFFECTIVE SPEAKER

Rate your current presentation skills (circle your answer).

Verbal

Excellent	**Good**	**Fair**	Clear message
Excellent	**Good**	**Fair**	Relevant to audience
Excellent	**Good**	**Fair**	Effective evidence
Excellent	**Good**	**Fair**	Powerful visual aids
Excellent	**Good**	**Fair**	Listener involvement
Excellent	**Good**	**Fair**	Good question-and-answer sessions

Visual

Excellent	**Good**	**Fair**	Making eye contact
Excellent	**Good**	**Fair**	Using gestures effectively
Excellent	**Good**	**Fair**	Using facial expressions

Vocal

Excellent	**Good**	**Fair**	Raising and lowering volume
Excellent	**Good**	**Fair**	Changing pace
Excellent	**Good**	**Fair**	Using pauses for emphasis

LESSON 2

DEFINE THE CENTRAL MESSAGE

Presentation:_____

Topic:

Central message:

LESSON 3

KNOW YOUR LISTENERS

Presentation:_____

Meaning of the message:

Goal:

Listener Analysis

Presentation:_____

What is their attitude toward me?

How can I convince them of my message?

How much do they know about the topic?

What are their positions?

How do they like to receive their information?

How are they responding to the information they're receiving?

LESSON 4

ENERGY FOR EFFECTIVENESS

Energy Evaluation

Presentation:_____

Techniques

Excellent	**Good**	**Fair**	**Poor**	Using gestures for description
Excellent	**Good**	**Fair**	**Poor**	Using gestures for emphasis
Excellent	**Good**	**Fair**	**Poor**	Using expansive gestures
Excellent	**Good**	**Fair**	**Poor**	Using facial expressions
Excellent	**Good**	**Fair**	**Poor**	Raising and lowering voice
Excellent	**Good**	**Fair**	**Poor**	Changing pacing
Excellent	**Good**	**Fair**	**Poor**	Using pauses for emphasis
Excellent	**Good**	**Fair**	**Poor**	Communicating with voice tone

LESSON 5

EYE-CONTACT COMMUNICATION

Eye-Contact Evaluation

Presentation:_____

Always	**Often**	**Seldom**	Did you use the three-step approach to eye contact?
Always	**Often**	**Seldom**	Did you avoid a regular pattern of eye contact?
Always	**Often**	**Seldom**	Did you use your eyes to control your pace?
Always	**Often**	**Seldom**	Did you use your eyes to get feedback from listeners?

LESSON 6

GATHER YOUR EVIDENCE

Evidence Checklist

Presentation:_____

Yes	**No**	Did you do mind-mapping or brainstorming?
Yes	**No**	Did you organize ideas according to the rule of threes?
Yes	**No**	Did you include a variety of evidence anecdotes, analogies, statistics, and so on?
Yes	**No**	Did you draw evidence from your own experience?
Yes	**No**	Did your evidence meet the five-C test?
Yes	**No**	Did you create a preliminary outline?

LESSON 7

ORGANIZE YOUR MATERIAL

Check the organizing pattern(s) you used.

Organizing Patterns

Presentation_____

- ❏ The whole and its parts
- ❏ Spatial order
- ❏ Chronological order
- ❏ News reporter
- ❏ Problem-solution
- ❏ Best alternative
- ❏ Other

LESSON 8

CREATE SUCCESSFUL PRESENTATIONS

Keys to Success

Presentation:_____

Yes	**No**	Did the opening hook listeners?
Yes	**No**	Did you organize the body effectively?
Yes	**No**	Did you transition the presentation body with summaries?
Yes	**No**	Did you close by repeating the central message?
Yes	**No**	Did you include a call to action?

Lesson 9

Interact with Audiences

Presentation:_____

How many dialogue questions did you include? _____

Were the questions open- or close-ended? _____

When did you ask the dialogue questions? _____

What did you accomplish with them? _____

Lesson 10

Visual Aids

Presentation:_____

How many visual aids did you have? _____

What kinds of visuals did you use? _____

Did you keep your visuals simple? _____

Was the information readable? _____

Was the design simple and effective? _____

How did listeners react to them? _____

Lesson 11

Presenting Your Visuals

Presentation:_____

What forms of visual aids did you use? _____

How well did they work with the talk? _____

Did you use the four-step process? _____

If so, was it effective? _____

How did you handle handouts? _____

Lesson 12

Make It Simple

Presentation:_____

Did you speak in a conversational style? _____

Did you use active voice as much as possible? _____

Did you avoid needless jargon? _____

Did you define any acronyms? _____

Did you avoid big words? _____

Did you remove nonwords from your talk? _____

Lesson 13

Banish those Butterflies

Presentation:_____

How nervous did you feel before the start of your talk? _____
_____

How did you deal with this problem? _____

How did you feel as you were speaking? _____

How did you control your nervousness? _____

How well did all these techniques work? _____

LESSON 14

DEALING WITH THE DETAILS

Presentation:_____

Yes	No	Did you double-check date, time, directions?
Yes	No	Do you have an appropriate room arrangement?
Yes	No	Is the room large enough for your audience?
Yes	No	Are refreshments available if you need them?
Yes	No	Did you bring backup audiovisual materials?
Yes	No	Did you try out the audiovisual equipment?
Yes	No	Did you try out the microphone in advance?

LESSON 15

TEN-POINT PRESENTATION PRIMER

Presentation:_____

Yes	No	As you began to speak, did you make eye contact?
Yes	No	Did you open up all channels of communication?
Yes	No	Did you create a rhythm in your delivery?
Yes	No	Were your gestures raising your energy level?
Yes	No	Did you use dialogue questions effectively?
Yes	No	Did you use silences when you needed them?
Yes	No	Did you use the audiovisual equipment properly?
Yes	No	Did you try to memorize your talk?

LESSON 16

HANDLING QUESTIONS AND ANSWERS

Presentation:_____

How well did you anticipate the questions? _____

How often did you use the five-step process? _____

If you left out any steps, which ones? _____

If you had hostile listeners, how did you deal with them? _____
_____

Did you stay in control of the entire question-and-answer session?
_____

LESSON 17

ONE-TO-ONE PRESENTATIONS

Presentation:_____

Yes   No   Did you present a clear central message?

Yes   No   Did you clarify the meaning of your message?

Yes   No   Did your evidence appeal to the listener?

Yes   No   Did you present any visual aids effectively?

Yes   No   Did you use energy to make the presentation?

Yes   No   Did you practice eye contact?

Yes   No   Did you handle questions successfully?

Yes   No   Did you remember to "ask for the order?"

Lesson 18

Listening

Presentation:_____

Always	**Sometimes**	**Seldom**	Did you listen to the words and "read between the lines?"
Always	**Sometimes**	**Seldom**	Did you pay attention to your listeners' body language?
Always	**Sometimes**	**Seldom**	Did you avoid making quick judgments about your listeners?
Always	**Sometimes**	**Seldom**	Did you prevent distractions from interrupting your listening?
Always	**Sometimes**	**Seldom**	Did you try to put yourself in the shoes of the audience?

Lesson 19

Make Meetings Matter

Meeting:_____

Yes	**No**	You developed a clear central message for the meeting.
Yes	**No**	You wrote out an agenda and circulated it in advance.
Yes	**No**	You invited only those people who were absolutely necessary.
Yes	**No**	You set strict time limits and kept the meeting short.
Yes	**No**	You infused the meeting with energy.
Yes	**No**	You encouraged participation, but kept the meeting on track.
Yes	**No**	You ended the meeting with an action plan.

LESSON 20

MASTERING THE MEDIA

Interview:_____

Yes   No   You delivered your central message.

Yes   No   You remembered to wear appropriate attire.

Yes   No   You looked at the interviewer, not at the camera.

Yes   No   You answered with specifics, avoiding jargon and unsupported claims.

Yes   No   You handled the questions calmly and didn't overreact or become emotional.

Yes   No   You used energy to enhance your message.

LESSON 21

CONTINUOUS IMPROVEMENT

Use the 10 strategies on the following list every day, and you'll see continuous improvement in your presentation skills.

1. Practice your skills in every situation.

2. Take advantage of each opportunity at work to give a presentation.

3. Start with low-risk work situations to practice your skills as a presenter.

4. Participate in volunteer activities and start speaking to groups.

5. Join groups, like Toastmasters, so you can improve your skills.

6. Enroll in presentation skills courses.

7. Read materials on public speaking to continually update your knowledge.

8. Watch other speakers to determine whether they use the three channels of communication.

9. Solicit feedback from your listeners regarding your strengths and weaknesses.

10. Give yourself an ovation every time you speak.

INDEX